FABRIC PAINTING

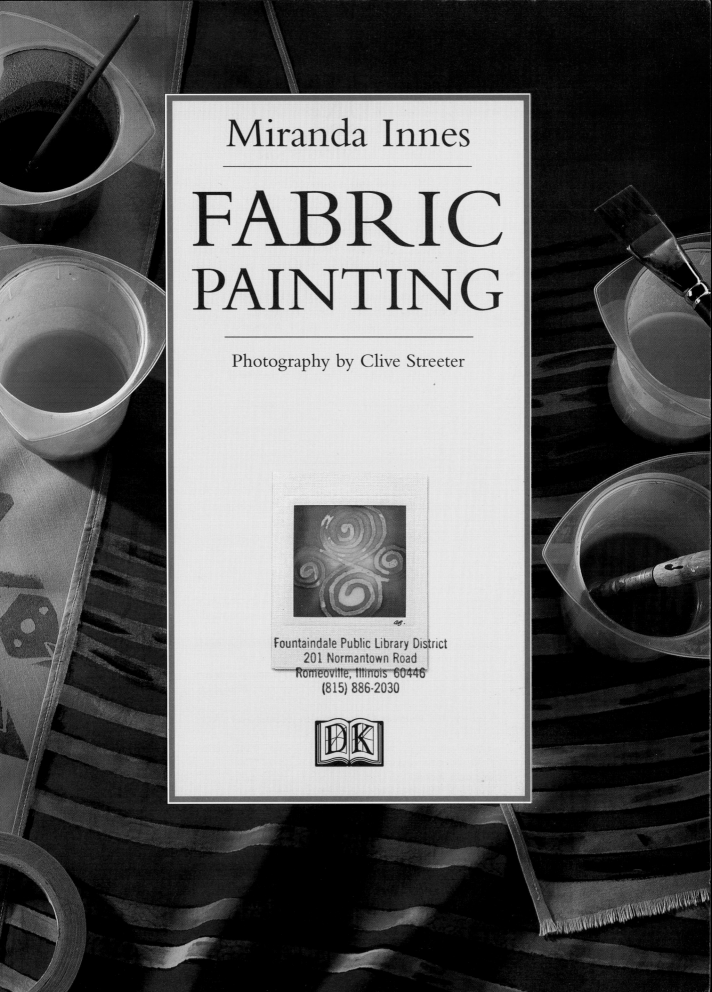

Miranda Innes

FABRIC PAINTING

Photography by Clive Streeter

DK

A DK PUBLISHING BOOK

Created and produced by
COLLINS & BROWN LIMITED
London House
Great Eastern Wharf
Parkgate Road
London SW11 4NQ

Project Editor	Heather Dewhurst
Managing Editor	Sarah Hoggett
Editorial Assistant	Corinne Asghar
Art Director	Roger Bristow
Art Editor	Marnie Searchwell
Photography	Clive Streeter
Stylist	Ali Edney

First American edition, 1996
2 4 6 8 10 9 7 5 3 1
Published in the United States by DK Publishing, Inc.
95 Madison Avenue, New York, NY 10016

Library of Congress Cataloging-in-Publication Data
Innes, Miranda.
    Fabric painting / by Miranda Innes. -- 1st American ed.
        p. cm. -- (Creative crafts)
    Includes index.
    ISBN 0-7894-0434-6
    1. Textile painting. 2. Silk painting. I. Title. II. Series:
Creative crafts (DK Publishing, Inc.)
TT851.I56 1996
746.6--dc20   95-42183
                                      CIP

Reproduced in Singapore by Daylight Colour Art
Printed and bound in France by Pollina - n° 68964 - B

Contents

Introduction 6

Basic Materials and Equipment 8

Basic Techniques 10

Painting and Dyeing

Introduction 12

Painted Jungle 14

Stylish Striped Silk 18

Bold Felt Blocks 22

Jousting Jumbos 26

Indigo and Rust 30

Velvet Magic 34

Ideas to Inspire 38

Printing

Introduction 42

Stenciled Heraldry 44

Leafy Sheer Silk 48

Easy Potato Print 52

Silk Screen Shells 56

Confetti Bright Silk 60

Seashore Canvas 64

Marbled Silk 68

Ideas to Inspire 72

Gutta and Wax-Resist

Introduction 76

Glowing Squares 78

Tropical Seascape 82

Aquatic Batik 86

Ideas to Inspire 90

Contributors 94

Index 95

Acknowledgments 96

Introduction

ONE FACTOR that sets humans apart from most other living things is that people love color and pattern. In the days when we wore nothing at all, we daubed our bodies with plant dyes or decorated our skin with patterns in henna or ash. When felt-making and weaving gave us something other than our own skins to wear, we decorated our garments with beads, shells, embroidery, and dyes, partly to proclaim rank, and partly because pattern and color are fundamental human needs and sources of joy.

Today, thanks to armies of people slaving over test tubes, we can apply color to almost everything we use. All kinds of fabric can be decorated in all sorts of ways, from the primitive magic of indigo-dipping, to the sheer chemical wizardry of pigments suspended in acrylic medium, which can be fixed, or set, with minimal equipment. Generally, there are just two types of fabric paint.

Chic Stripes
A stylish scarf painted with bands of yellow, brown, and pink dye.

Inking Up
Screen-printing ink is liberally applied with a spatula to ink up a sponge.

The first is water-based, which you set with an iron (a cautious hot iron pressed carefully on the reverse side of the fabric for a couple of minutes). This is a paint, and it lies on the surface of the fiber. The second type is known as fiber-reactive, and this requires professional steaming to set the color. Fiber-reactive color (also called steam-fixed or acid dye) is a dye, and penetrates right through the fiber.

Iron-set water-based paints do have a tendency to stiffen the fabric somewhat, although this may actually soften with time and washing. Water-based paints are readily available, easy to use and set, nontoxic, and perfect for use by children. They are fine for any natural fiber, such as cotton, silk, and linen.

Fiber-reactive dyes are excellent for protein-based fabrics, such as silk, wool, feathers, and nylon. They appear to be more lustrous and they flow more easily than water-based paints. Because they are dyes, they will color right through the fabric. Those

Fishy Theme
Underwater motifs were the inspiration for this framed batik.

dyes that are fiber-reactive do have one or two disadvantages, though. They are harder to locate, they require more in the way of chemicals and paraphernalia, and people are often allergic to them. Also, professional steamers are expensive, and it can be a nuisance to have to find a company that will steam your fabric for you – although you might find a textile design school near you that will allow you to use its steamer. Alternatively, there are some chemical dye-fixes available which obviate the need for steam-fixing, but you need to take care that you use the appropriate dye for the type of fix. After steaming, the color of fiber-reactive dye will change; it is not very lightfast, and it is liable to fade in sunlight. Dry-cleaning the dyed fabric is a proven way of preserving the dyed color.

There are three methods of controlling the spread of color on fabric. First, for a graphic design with strong outlines, you can use gutta or wax-resist. Second, for a wash of color, you can use antifusant or primer (which should relate to the specific type of fabric paint or dye you are using). Spread it

Spots and Squares
A floaty chiffon scarf is vibrantly patterned with bold blocks and spots of orange and red acid dye.

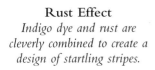

Rust Effect
Indigo dye and rust are cleverly combined to create a design of startling stripes.

liberally and evenly over the fabric with a wide brush or sponge. This produces a surface like paper, upon which you can paint and draw. Third, for a painterly finish more like oil paint, you can use a thickener combined with your color; this makes an ideal medium for such decorating techniques as printing, stenciling, and sponging. You can use any kind of brush to color your fabric. Alternatively, you could try using cotton balls, cotton swabs, or even an old sponge.

Begin fabric painting with just a few colors, or buy a kit. Start small, cheap, and manageable until you get the hang of it, and then discover the enormous pleasure of transforming both your home and your wardrobe with big, bold, and colorful patterns. Above all, do not be frightened. Improvise, experiment, and enjoy yourself.

Finally, a warning: when using any kind of chemical or powder, wear gloves and a protective mask, and work in a very well-ventilated room. Follow the manufacturer's instructions and do not mix elements from different methods: stick to either water-based or fiber-reactive colors and use all the ingredients from the same brand.

Neat Pleats
Pleating and folding fabric is a simple way to create patterns.

Basic Materials and Equipment

BEFORE YOU COMMENCE painting or dyeing, you should first wash and iron the fabric to be colored. Most fabrics are treated with finishing agents, which prevent ready absorption of paint and dye, and these need to be removed. When working with paint and dye, remember to wear your oldest clothes (rubber gloves and a protective mask are also necessary for some fabric dyes) and protect all work surfaces from the inevitable paint and dye spills.

Make sure your painting surface is flat; a kitchen table is ideal. Spread a plastic sheet over the table and tape it down. Then stretch a blanket or cotton sheet over the top and tape this down. Check that the fabric to be colored is wrinkle-free, then lay it over the padded surface and secure it with pins.

Thumbtacks

Silk pins

Claw pins

Masking tape

◀ Adhesive Tapes
Use masking tape to attach fabric to your surface; it can also be used to mask off areas of fabric when painting. Brown gummed tape is required when screen printing. Stick moistened tape around the edges of the screen mesh to prevent ink from seeping through.

▲ Pins and Tacks
Use thumbtacks or silk pins to pin your stretched fabric to a wooden frame for silk painting or batik. If you are painting a narrow strip of fabric, secure it to the frame with claw pins.

▼ Brushes
You can use any brushes you like for painting fabric. Sponge brushes are good for washes; artist's brushes are good for detailing.

▼ Pens and Markers
Sketch your designs with pencils, pastels, or felt-tip pens. Use tailor's chalk for marking fabric. Silk outline markers, as their name suggests, can be used to draw on silk.

Brown gummed tape

Felt-tip pen

Assorted paintbrushes

Sponge brush

Tailor's chalk

Silk outline marker

Pastel

Pencil

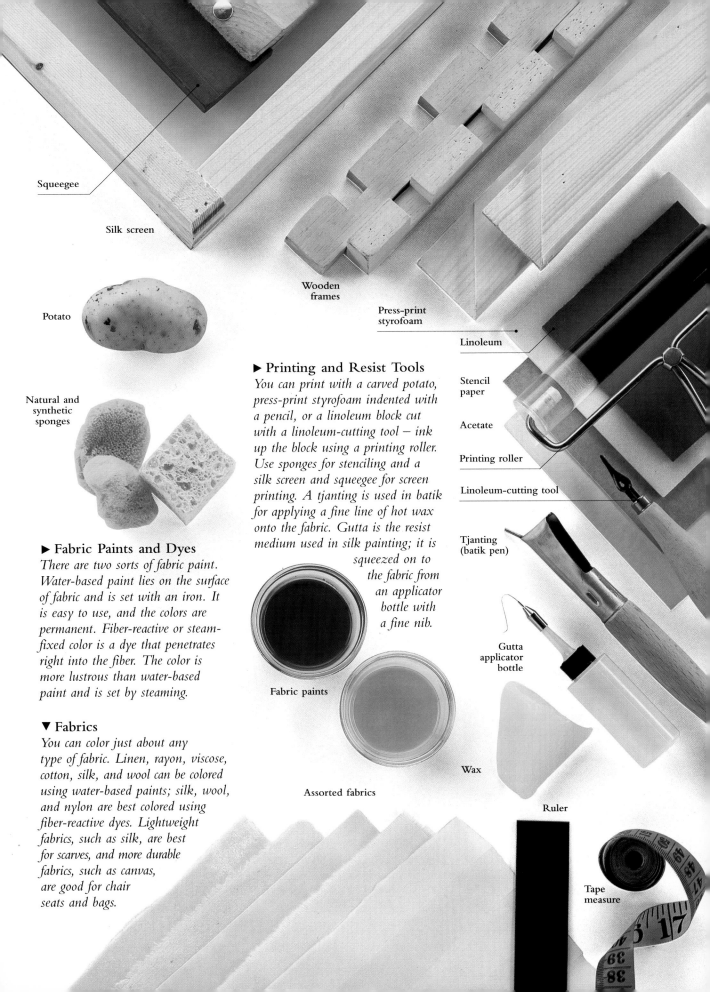

Squeegee

Silk screen

Potato

Natural and synthetic sponges

Wooden frames

Press-print styrofoam

Linoleum

Stencil paper

Acetate

Printing roller

Linoleum-cutting tool

Tjanting (batik pen)

Gutta applicator bottle

Wax

Ruler

Tape measure

Fabric paints

Assorted fabrics

▶ Printing and Resist Tools

You can print with a carved potato, press-print styrofoam indented with a pencil, or a linoleum block cut with a linoleum-cutting tool — ink up the block using a printing roller. Use sponges for stenciling and a silk screen and squeegee for screen printing. A tjanting is used in batik for applying a fine line of hot wax onto the fabric. Gutta is the resist medium used in silk painting; it is squeezed on to the fabric from an applicator bottle with a fine nib.

▶ Fabric Paints and Dyes

There are two sorts of fabric paint. Water-based paint lies on the surface of fabric and is set with an iron. It is easy to use, and the colors are permanent. Fiber-reactive or steam-fixed color is a dye that penetrates right into the fiber. The color is more lustrous than water-based paint and is set by steaming.

▼ Fabrics

You can color just about any type of fabric. Linen, rayon, viscose, cotton, silk, and wool can be colored using water-based paints; silk, wool, and nylon are best colored using fiber-reactive dyes. Lightweight fabrics, such as silk, are best for scarves, and more durable fabrics, such as canvas, are good for chair seats and bags.

Basic Techniques

THERE ARE MANY different techniques of coloring fabric, of which screen printing is one of the more complex. Screen printing is a method of printing a design on fabric using a fine mesh screen held in a wooden frame (see below). Ink is pressed through a stencil on the screen mesh using a flexible rubber blade (squeegee) to print onto the fabric. You can print using a paper stencil taped to the screen (see p. 58) or a photo stencil exposed on your screen (see p. 28). The latter is more involved and expensive, but the resulting print is crisper, and the stencil lasts much longer.

Screen Printing

To obtain a photo stencil, first photocopy your chosen design onto acetate. (Feed the acetate through the photocopier by hand; using automatic feed could melt the acetate.) Take the acetate and your screen to a printer who can transfer the design photographically onto your screen. This photo stencil will remain permanently on your screen until you choose to remove or change it.

When the stencil is in place, moisten brown gummed tape and stick it around all four edges of the screen mesh. Position the screen on the fabric so the mesh is in contact with the fabric, and align any registration marks (see below). Spoon ink along the top edge of the screen, farthest away from you. Place the squeegee in the ink and pull it across the screen toward you, pressing firmly and evenly to push the ink through the area of the stencil in the mesh. When you reach the edge nearest you, push the squeegee back across the screen to the top again. Lift up the screen and wash it, using a sponge and cold water to remove all traces of ink. If ink is left to dry on the screen, the mesh will become clogged and unusable.

If you are repeating a motif, you can mark your screen with pencil marks at the edges to

Making a Silk Screen

1 Using a backsaw and mitering block, saw a length of wood into four equal pieces. Cut the end of one piece to a mitered corner; cut the other end so its mitered corner runs in the opposite direction. Repeat with the remaining three pieces.

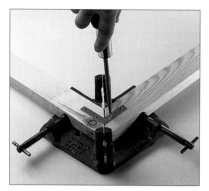

2 Sand the corners, then glue them with wood glue. Assemble the pieces into a frame, and clamp each corner in a corner clamp to set. Screw a right-angled bracket into each corner for extra strength. Leave the frame to dry for approximately 12 hours.

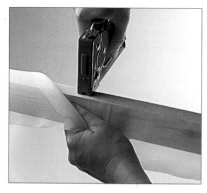

3 Paint two coats of boat varnish on the frame, allowing the first coat to dry before applying the next. Stretch a piece of silk mesh over the back of the frame, and staple one edge of the silk down all along one side of the wood to secure.

correspond to the edges of the motif. These are called registration marks. Align the marks on the screen with the printed pattern on the fabric before printing again. Alternatively, you can line up images by eye, although this method is not as accurate.

Making a Repeat Pattern

One method of making a repeat pattern is to draw the motif on a piece of paper using a black felt-tip pen, then photocopy it several times; alternatively, you could photocopy a printed image. Carefully cut out the motifs and arrange them on paper to make a repeat pattern. Lay a sheet of acetate over the paper and trace the pattern onto the acetate using an opaque black pen. The photo stencil can be made from this acetate, as above.

For a repeating abstract pattern, first draw a busy pattern to fill a square or rectangular area. Cut vertically through the center of the design in a wavy line. Transpose the two halves of the design, so the wavy edges are on the outside; tape the two halves together on the reverse side. Cut horizontally through the center of the design in a wavy line. Transpose

the two halves and tape them together on the reverse. The design should now have four wavy edges. Photocopy this several times. Cut out the copies and stick them together, matching the wavy edges exactly; the pattern should repeat to make one continuous pattern. Photocopy this onto acetate to make a photo stencil, as above.

Fixing Paints and Dyes

Most paints and dyes need to be fixed onto the fabric, either by ironing or by steaming, to prevent the colors from running when the fabric is washed. Always follow the manufacturer's instructions.

To steam your fabric, you will need to obtain a steamer or find a company that will steam the fabric for you; alternatively, you can steam a small piece of fabric in a pressure cooker. Place the fabric on a piece of cotton and roll up the layers together. Tuck the ends in and pin to secure. Pour ¾–1¼in (2–3cm) of water in the pressure cooker. Place the roll in a metal basket and suspend it above the water. Cover the basket with paper and foil, then seal the lid and cook for 45 minutes.

4 *Pull the mesh over the front of the frame so it is taut and wrinkle-free, and staple it securely to the frame on the remaining sides. You may need to enlist the help of another pair of hands for this stage.*

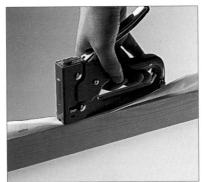

5 *Fold over any excess ends of the mesh on all sides to neaten the screen. Staple the folded ends to the frame sides. If the mesh is ever damaged, simply undo the staples, unfold and reposition the spare mesh, and staple it onto the frame again.*

6 *Stick moistened brown gummed tape around all four edges of the screen mesh, on the side on which you will be applying the ink. This will prevent any ink from seeping down between the edges of the mesh and the wooden frame, and ruining the design.*

Painting and Dyeing

·····································

WHETHER YOU ARE using a bucket of farmyard-fragrant indigo or a housepainter's brush dripping with fiber-reactive dye, painting and dyeing fabric is a primitive pleasure that can quickly and easily produce textiles of classic simplicity or contemporary sophistication. You can transform all kinds of fabric, from fine silk *habutae* to soft felt or coarse canvas, and you can decorate anything from a delicate scarf to a cozy rug. Fabric painting and dyeing is the easiest introduction to color and requires very little in the way of equipment. Everything you produce in this way is unique and will have a lively texture and character. A simple design is often the best; your first project could be a fine silk scarf painted with nothing more complicated than wide stripes of orange and scarlet.

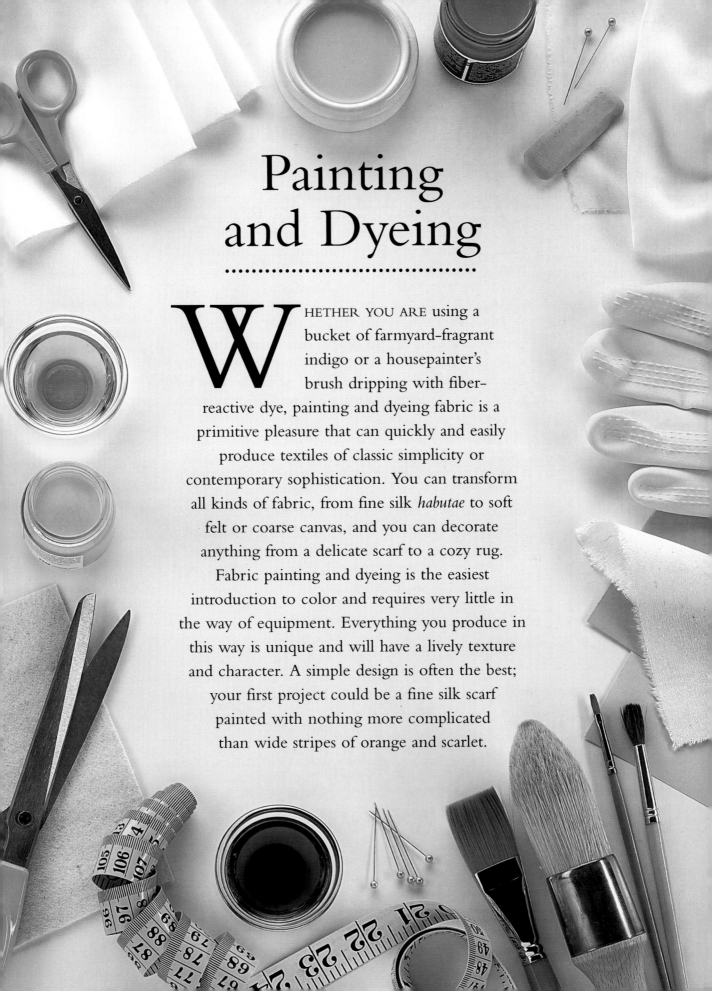

Painted Jungle

MATERIALS
Colored paper
Pastels
Cotton fabric
Premixed
pigment dyes

EQUIPMENT
Scissors
Iron
Absorbent fabric
Masking tape
Artist's brush

A PAINTERLY CROSS between the work of Rousseau and Matisse, this blind is most likely to appeal to the extrovert. The lively freehand shapes are fun to paint, relying more on panache than precision, and the finished blind is a great way to give terrific impact to your windows for the price of a length of muslin.

The design starts life like a child's scrapbook, playing with colors and simple paper shapes; in this way, the layout can be worked out in miniature before committing to the large scale. Instead of jungle leaves, you could paint a school of striped fish to adorn a bathroom, or yellow daisies to brighten a kitchen. You could use a stencil for repeatability, or apply the color with a sponge for a stippled texture.

When making the blind, bear in mind that you will need to make side turnings, and allow an extra few inches in the width of fabric for this. You will also need to allow extra for the hem and blind roller. After you have made the blind, you can protect your artwork by spraying it with blind stiffener, which may also cause it to shrink slightly.

Blind Devotion
A scattering of bright leaves is the perfect antidote to a depressing view. The horticulturally minded might like to paint an herb collection for their kitchen windows. Doting parents could create a meadow full of little ponies, while lepidopterists can attempt fluttering purple emperors and painted ladies.

New Leaves
Elements of the same design are here given a very different look with a different range of color. Experiment with colored paper, and paint your blind to match your decor.

Painting the Fabric

Using your cut paper shapes as a rough guide, take a deep breath and pick up your brush. The raw materials will not break the bank, so loosen up and enjoy yourself.

Pastels and colored paper

Cotton fabric

Premixed pigment dyes

1 *Plan your design by drawing motifs on paper, using colored paper to match the colors of dye you plan to use. Using pastels will help create the effect of brushstrokes. Cut out all the motifs.*

2 *Arrange the cut-out motifs on a piece of paper until you like the design. This bold design is based on leaf motifs. The paper template will provide a reference to follow when you begin painting.*

3 *To avoid uneven shrinkage, wash, dry, and iron the cotton fabric before you start to paint. Lay the fabric over a piece of absorbent fabric on a work surface. Stretch it taut and tape it to the surface with masking tape. Practice painting a few brushstrokes on a spare piece of fabric. When you are confident, begin to paint the motifs using premixed pigment dyes.*

4 *Gradually build up the pattern, painting outlines first, then filling in the shapes with contrasting colors. The technique of handpainting lends itself to bold, simple shapes, as here, and bright colors look most effective. Paint the large shapes first to determine the structure of the design, then add smaller leaf motifs in the spaces.*

5 *When the basic shapes of the design are painted, continue to fill in any white areas in between with bold dabs and brushstrokes of color. Here, blue and yellowish green dye are painted on to the fabric in a loose representation of tufts of grass.*

6 *When you have finished painting, let the fabric dry. Then set the colors by running an iron, at a medium temperature, over the fabric, moving the iron constantly to avoid leaving marks on the fabric.*

7 *The finished fabric is now ready to be made into a window blind. Any remaining fabric can be used to make matching pillow covers.*

Stylish Striped Silk

MATERIALS

Sandwashed silk
Masking tape
Acid dyes mixed with thickener (following manufacturer's instructions)
Water
Mild detergent

EQUIPMENT

Scissors
Tape measure
Housepainter's brush
Hair dryer (optional)
Artist's brush
Cotton fabric
Steamer

STRONG AND UNEXPECTED COLORS are boldly combined with crisp graphic stripes in a scarf that is as elegant as it is simple. Deep vibrant blue, the color of a tropical night sky, makes a sizzling contrast to hand-painted bands of acid yellow, warm terra-cotta, and cerulean. Masking tape is a simple material for giving a sharply defined resist pattern, acheived by blocking off the dye; it is very easy to mask off straight-sided geometric shapes. The contrasting border is a simple and effective finishing touch. A steady hand to apply the color is useful, but not essential; the impact of the design does not rely as much on exact precision as on bold contrast.

The dense, rich color, tactile feel, and opulent drape of the finished scarf come from using heavy sandwashed silk. This entails painting the design twice, on front and back, since the fabric is too heavy for the dye to penetrate. If this seems too daunting, you can use lighter silk, which can be painted all at once, and achieve a floaty scarf with brilliant color.

Sharp Scarf
Uneven stripes of painterly color give this scarf a cool, clean, contemporary look, with just a hint of 1930s elegance. This is a definite designer item, to be worn with white linen and panache.

Massed Bands
There is no need to keep your stripes symmetrical, or to confine them to one direction. As you become adept, you may prefer to dispense with masking tape altogether in favor of a looser freehand style.

Painting the Silk
With a roll of masking tape, a chunky paintbrush,
and your acid dyes at hand, you can indulge in an orgy
of brilliant, undiluted color.

Masking tape and sandwashed silk

Acid dyes mixed with thickener

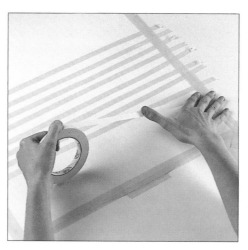

1 *Cut a length of sandwashed silk the size of a scarf. Stretch the silk over the work surface and secure all sides with masking tape. Stick masking tape from side to side across the width of the fabric, spacing the strips about 1in (2.5cm) apart for approximately 12in (30cm) at each end. Do not worry about making the taped lines absolutely straight and even; uneven lines add to the overall design.*

2 *Test the dye on a spare piece of fabric to check the coloring. Using a house-painter's brush, paint blue dye over the surface of the silk. Paint from right to left for an even effect, or add curving brushstrokes for texture. Leave the fabric to dry for 30 minutes, or use a hair dryer to speed up the drying time. Peel off the horizontal strips of masking tape to reveal white stripes beneath (see inset).*

3 *Using a fine artist's brush, paint the four white stripes nearest the middle of the fabric with a mixture of blue and black dyes. Then paint the rest of the white stripes with yellow dye; this will look orange when wet.*

4 *Paint details on the stripes for added color and texture. Here, streaks and dabs of pink dye are painted on to the orange-yellow stripes. Leave the silk to dry naturally for about 30 minutes, or use a hair dryer.*

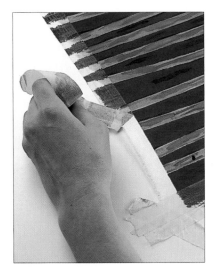

5 *Peel off the masking tape on the outer edges of the fabric. Since the dye has not yet reached this part of the fabric, it will still be white.*

6 *Paint the outer border with yellow dye to match the stripes and contrast with the blue of the fabric. Leave the silk for 30 minutes to dry completely, or dry with a hair dryer.*

7 *Turn the fabric over. The dye will show through in patches on the underside. (If you use a finer silk, the dye will penetrate through completely.) Mask off the stripes and border, as before, and paint the underside of the fabric to match the front. Let dry.*

8 *Lay the painted silk flat. Place a piece of cotton fabric on top, and roll up the silk with the cotton inside (this will prevent any part of the painted silk from touching another part and causing the dyes to run). Steam the silk for 45 minutes to set the dyes. Rinse with cold water; then, if the water is still not running clear, wash with mild detergent. Rinse again and let dry.*

Bold Felt Blocks

MATERIALS

Heavy wool felt

Acid dyes mixed with thickener (following manufacturer's instructions)

Water

Mild detergent

EQUIPMENT

Masking tape

Tailor's chalk

Metal ruler

Selection of paintbrushes

Hair dryer

Backing cloth

Steamer

Tumble dryer

THIS RUG IS NOT A SHRINKING VIOLET; it is bold, brash, and very beautiful. It is also wonderfully warm and comforting, and the perfect antidote to cold, gray winter weather. The elements of the pattern are as basic as can be – just blocks and stripes with a childish finger-painting repertoire of blobs, wavy lines, and squiggles. But they combine in an extraordinarily effective and dramatic way to make a throw rug that would be a handsome addition to either a sleek modern sofa or a rustic farmhouse bedroom.

The irregular freehand design of this throw rug is strangely enhanced by its apparently arbitrary layout; you will have to set aside any notions of symmetry and neatness if you want to capture the spontaneous liveliness of this project. Using large paintbrushes helps banish tendencies toward prissiness. Likewise, the confident use of an unusual color combination is something to copy; it is all too easy to aim for good taste and end up with a bland design. The heavy felt fabric soaks up color like a sponge and is as stiff as a board until it is steamed, yet the finished result has the soft, matte richness of suede.

Winning Throw
Banded, bordered, and multifariously patterned with patches of bright color, this is a throw rug with tremendous verve, yet it is surprisingly easy to make.

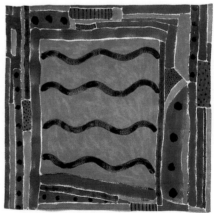

Stunningly Spotted
These wool throw rugs have been given a looser freehand treatment than the main design. The brushstrokes here are more obvious, contributing to the vigorous design.

Painting the Felt

*Take your courage in both hands — the size of this throw
rug is its most daunting aspect. Painting it is child's play.
Do not worry if the colors are dull when they dry,
because steaming brings out their richness.*

Heavy wool felt

Acid dyes mixed
with thickener

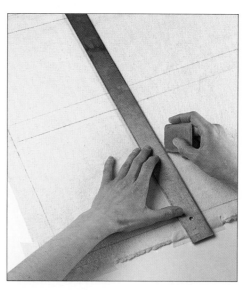

1 *Attach the heavy wool felt to the work
surface with masking tape along the edges
so it lies flat. Mark out the design on the
fabric using tailor's chalk and a metal ruler.
This design is composed of squares and blocks.*

2 *Paint dye on to the fabric, a section
at a time. Since the fabric is so thick,
brushstrokes will not be visible, so you can
paint in any direction.*

3 *Continue painting on more colors to fill in the
outlines of the pattern on the fabric. Do not worry
if some colors bleed into each other at adjoining edges,
because this adds to the overall effect.*

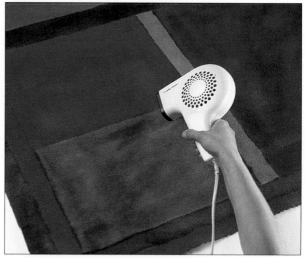

4 *Remove the masking tape from the edges of the fabric
and paint the edges. Then dry the fabric with a hair
dryer. Because wool felt is so heavy, it would take several
days to dry naturally.*

5 *Paint details on the fabric in black dye. Use a large, round-ended paintbrush to make large random blobs.*

6 *Use a smaller artist's brush to paint curly squiggles and small dots. Allow the fabric to dry again, either naturally or with the help of a hair dryer.*

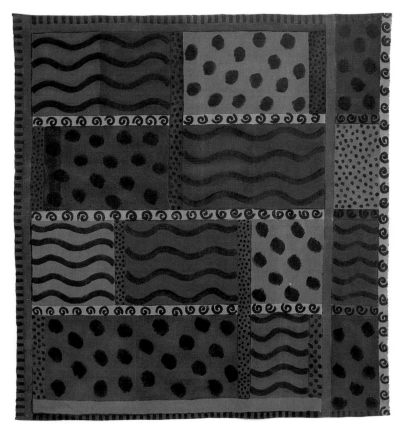

7 *Wrap the fabric in a backing cloth and steam it for 45 minutes to set the dyes. Rinse in cold water until the water runs clear, then wash it in mild detergent and rinse again. Tumble-dry the fabric, then let it dry completely.*

Jousting Jumbos

MATERIALS
Paper
Acetate
Silk *habutae*
Brown gummed tape
Cold-water fiber-
reactive dyes
Water
Mild detergent

EQUIPMENT
Colored crayons
Photocopier
Paper glue
Opaque black pen
Screen
Absorbent fabric
Masking tape
Squeegee
Sponge
Steamer
Iron
Artist's brush
Dye bath
Rubber gloves

LAYERS OF COLOR give this printed and hand-painted silk a luminous vibrancy and energy. Curiously, although the initial dyes are blue, they are altered by the alchemy of the scarlet dye into lively patches of a darker but indeterminate color. This is one of the mysteries of fabric coloring, and one of the reasons it is such a fascinating art. Pastels are a useful means to explore color possibilities; they are as brilliant as dyes, and you can layer them to achieve approximate color mixes.

These tussling trunks and tusks are printed at random on heavy silk using a photo stencil (see p.10). You can trace any image, as simple or as complex as you have patience for, and repeat it as often as you wish, adding shading or heavier outlines where you would like to emphasize certain aspects of the design. Widely spaced and vigorously painted like this, the design becomes almost abstract and part of the general rich texture; a paler or more even dye would make the black drawings more obvious. The temptation when painting is to be too exact, but in this case precision is an enemy of spontaneity, so aim to be loose and free with your brushstrokes.

Dyed Tie
Scarlet silk elephants make a welcome change from standard designs for business ties, and they have an impressive painterly quality. Beware, however, of anything verging toward pink in the elephant line.

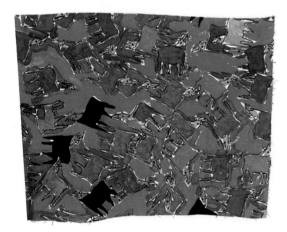 

Colored Creatures
It is not necessary to dip-dye your fabric — these creatures were hand-painted in random patches of color: the goats in fairly translucent color, the elephants in intense cobalt and scarlet.

Coloring the Silk

*This project is your chance to try your hand at
everything: the crisp precision of photo stencils, the lively texture
of handpainting, and the unifying intensity of dipdyeing.*

Acetate and paper

Silk *habutae*

Cold-water fiber-
reactive dyes

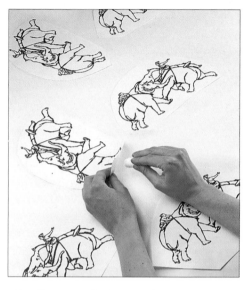

1 *Using different sources for reference, draw a design for your fabric. Here the design is based on elephants, but you could choose a simpler motif. Experiment with different color families using crayons or pastels.*

2 *Photocopy the design; glue copies on paper in a repeat pattern. Trace on to acetate with an opaque black pen. Take the acetate and a screen (see p. 10) to a printer, who will make a photo stencil (see p. 10).*

3 *Stretch a piece of silk habutae over absorbent fabric on a work surface, securing with masking tape. Stick moistened brown gummed tape around the edges of the mesh and the wooden frame on the screen, and position the screen on the fabric (see p. 10). Spoon black dye paste on to the top edge of the screen and print on the fabric (see p. 10). Repeat along the fabric. Wash the screen thoroughly.*

4 *Steam the fabric for 20 minutes to set the dye (see p. 10), then wash it out with cold water until the water runs clear. Wash and rinse again. Dry and iron the silk. Tape it over the printing surface so it is taut. Using an artist's brush and pale blue dye, dab random brushstrokes around the motifs. The brushstrokes will be visible in the finished piece, adding extra texture.*

5 Let the fabric dry, then paint on dark blue dye in random patches, filling in more of the background color and some of the motifs. Again, paint in different directions to leave plenty of visible brushstrokes. Steam and wash the fabric as in step 4 to set the dye.

6 Prepare a dye bath of red dye, following the manufacturer's instructions. Wearing rubber gloves for protection, immerse the painted silk in the dye bath. Simmer for 15 minutes, stirring constantly to ensure an even distribution of color. Pull the fabric out, and rinse in cold water until the water runs clear.

7 Wash the fabric with mild detergent and rinse again until the water runs clear. Let the fabric dry, and iron it to finish. The dyed and printed fabric is now ready to be made into a tie.

Indigo and Rust

MATERIALS

Indigo dye (made from soda ash, water, sodium hydrosulfite, and indigo grains)

Silk noil

Mild liquid detergent

Masking tape

Strong nylon thread

Ferrous sulfate crystals

Water

Fast Black K salt

Fabric softener

EQUIPMENT

Protective mask

Bucket with lid

Plastic wrap

Iron

Rubber gloves

2 paintbrushes

INDIGO MUST BE THE MOST universal dye, and one of the most mysterious. Quite apart from the overpowering smell, nothing beats the strange alchemy of indigo and oxygen that transforms white cloth into the most heavenly blue. Indigo is also one of the least noxious dye ingredients, as are ferrous sulfate (or rust) and Fast Black K salt.

In Africa, indigo dye is kept in pits in the ground, and lively resist patterns are drawn on to the fabric with cassava paste to resist the dye, preventing it from penetrating the fabric; in Malaysia, complex wax-resist designs are drawn with a penlike instrument called a *tjanting*. Our project shows a sophisticated version of tie-dyeing that owes much to the inspiration of Japanese textiles, and nothing to the psychedelic tie-dyed T-shirts of the 1960s. Generally, tie-dyeing is a technique to adopt with extreme caution. In India, the dyers make thousands of tiny knots in traditional patterns, such as delicate constellations of fireworks, and the finished effect is divine. This requires time and years of experience, which most amateurs do not have. However, tie-dyeing fabric in carefully folded stripes is relatively easy to do, and produces a result that is both original and elegant.

Muted Blues
A stylish scarf combining simplicity with elegance. The blue darkens the more often it is dipped in indigo and exposed to the air. One of the advantages of using these nonchemical dyes is that the fabric does not have to be boiled or steamed to set the color, which might damage some fine fabrics.

Ties to Dye For
The primitive techniques of folding, tying, dyeing, and painting give interestingly unpredictable results. These examples show the subtle color range that can be achieved using just three dye substances.

Dyeing the Silk

Indigo dyeing is not for the impatient or the overly fastidious. It is an earthy, organic process, which is kind to the planet and has a magic unlike any other.

Silk noil

Indigo dye,
ferrous sulfate, and
Fast Black K salt

Masking tape and
strong nylon thread

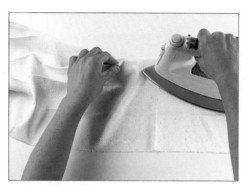

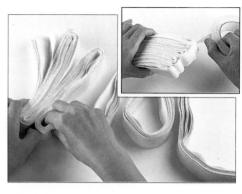

1 *Wearing a mask, prepare the indigo dye. Mix 9 teaspoons (40g) soda ash in a bucket half-filled with hand-hot water. Stir in 5 teaspoons (20g) sodium hydrosulfite and 5 teaspoons (20g) indigo grains. Fill the bucket with hot water, cover with plastic wrap and a lid, and leave for two hours. Wash the silk noil in mild detergent. When dry, pleat it with 2in (5cm) pleats. Iron along the folds.*

2 *Fold the pleated fabric in a snakelike fashion to form a bunch of folds about 6in (15cm) long. Wrap masking tape around the outer edges of the bunch to contain the folded sections (see inset).*

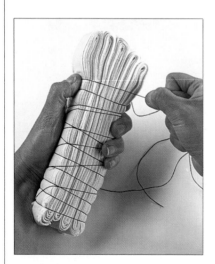

3 *Starting in the center, bind the taped bunch with strong nylon thread, wrapping the thread around and around the bunch along its entire length, leaving ½in (12mm) between each strand. Tie the two ends of the thread together to secure. The tighter the thread ends are tied, the more pronounced will be the pattern.*

4 *Wearing rubber gloves, dip the bound fabric in the bucket of indigo dye and hold it there for 10 seconds. Then lift it out for 2 minutes, during which time the dye will turn completely blue. Dip it in for another 10 seconds and lift it out again.*

5 *Untie the thread and unwrap the masking tape from the fabric. Open the fabric to reveal a dramatic change of color. The fabric will be covered with bright yellow stripes for a few seconds before the dye reacts with the oxygen in the air.*

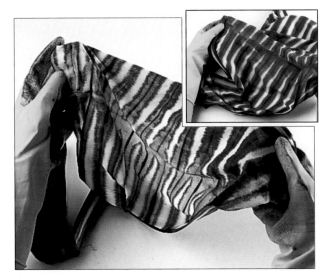

6 After a few seconds the color of the dye will change to green, and then, a few seconds later, to blue (see inset). The color change from yellow to blue takes only about 30 seconds. Let the fabric dry, rinse it, and let dry again. Then pleat the fabric again, this time at an angle. Repeat the stages of binding, dipping, and rinsing.

7 Squeeze out the excess water from the fabric and lay it on a flat surface. Mix 2 teaspoons (10g) ferrous sulfate crystals with 2 cups (500ml) hot water to dissolve the crystals. Paint streaks of ferrous sulfate solution over the wet fabric; this will turn the fabric yellow. Mix 1 teaspoon (5g) Fast Black K salt with 2 cups (500ml) cold water to create a blue-colored solution, and paint streaks of this over the fabric, which will produce burgundy colors (see inset).

8 Let the fabric dry, then rinse it, first in cold and then in warm water. Wash it in mild liquid detergent and rinse until the color stops running. Give the fabric a final rinse with fabric softener and let dry. It is now ready to be made into a scarf.

Velvet Magic

MATERIALS

Silk velvet
Masking tape
Acid dyes
Water
Discharge dye
Mild detergent

EQUIPMENT

Absorbent natural
fabric
Housepainter's brush
Hair dryer (optional)
Screen with photo
stencil
Squeegee
Sponge
Plastic bottle
with nozzle
Plastic discharge
applicator bottle
Pins
Backing cloth
Steamer
Iron

ONE OF THE GREATEST PLEASURES of fabric painting is that you cannot always foresee exactly what you will end up with – this opulent silk velvet pillow is a case in point. Its glowing base color is enriched and intensified by several layers of closely toning warmer reds, and bold emphases in black contribute a sharp counterpoint. The fabric, at this stage, is powerful, but the effect is somewhat heavy, and this is where the magic of discharge dye comes in. The leavening action of this bleaching dye takes place during steaming.

Discharge dyes are not pleasant to use, and as with all dyes, you must be cautious about handling them and breathing in fumes. The effort is well repaid, however, with an exciting result that cannot be achieved in any other way. The bleached spots and squares of warm biscuit beige make a perfect, but unexpected, contrast to the rest of the colors.

One of the strengths of this powerful fabric design lies in its use of simple geometric elements that are boldly juxtaposed. Much of its impact, however, derives from the use of a strong, but related, color palette. Carefully considered restraint is aesthetically, as well as economically, more effective.

Pillowed Comfort
Silk velvet catches the light in a fascinating way – with a halo of brightness contrasted with inky shadows.
The shining, saturated colors come across hypercharged with intensity. Go for the glow!

Moody Blues
Oranges are not the only color – night skies and stormy seas suggest alternatives. And pillows are not the only project – think of sinuous, sumptuous shawls and scarves.

Painting the Velvet

This pillow cover is simply fabulous, with a nice balance between formal and spontaneous. Copy this design exactly and you will have a pillow to be proud of, as well as a head full of ideas for alternative designs and colors.

Silk velvet

Acid dyes

Masking tape and discharge dye

1 *Stretch a piece of silk velvet (with the nap facing upward) over absorbent natural fabric on a work surface, and secure it to the surface with masking tape. Using a house-painter's brush, paint orange acid dye on the fabric in a bold abstract design, leaving some areas of the fabric unpainted.*

2 *Paint red dye overlapping the base color, covering more of the velvet. It does not matter if the colors merge. The colors will not bleed as much with the thick velvet as they would on thin fabric. Any merging of colors actually adds to the effect.*

3 *Continue to build up the layers of color on the velvet, this time using a darker red. Use this color to emphasize the basic shapes in the design by filling in the background. The velvet should now be completely covered with dye. Leave the fabric to dry overnight, or speed up the process by using a hair dryer.*

4 *Using a screen with a geometric photo stencil (see p.28), print more blocks of color over the fabric (see p.10). Because the velvet nap is so thick, you should repeat this process about six times for an even print. Carefully lift up the screen to reveal the printed image on the velvet. Wash the screen with a sponge and cold water.*

5 *Using a plastic bottle filled with black acid dye, squeeze out dots and lines through the nozzle onto the fabric for additional decoration. Let the fabric dry overnight. Cover part of the fabric with crisscrossing lines of masking tape. Paint discharge dye through the masked area (see inset). Remove the tape.*

6 *Using a plastic discharge applicator bottle, paint discharge dye circles elsewhere on the fabric. The discharge dye will only look wet here. When the fabric is steamed, the discharge bleaches out the color beneath it. Dry the fabric using a hair dryer on a cool setting. It is best to steam the fabric on the same day.*

7 *Pin the velvet onto a backing cloth, and roll it up with the cloth inside to keep the colors from running. Steam for an hour to set the dyes, and let dry. Wash the fabric in cold water with mild detergent; rinse until the water runs clear. When dry, iron on the reverse side.*

Ideas to Inspire

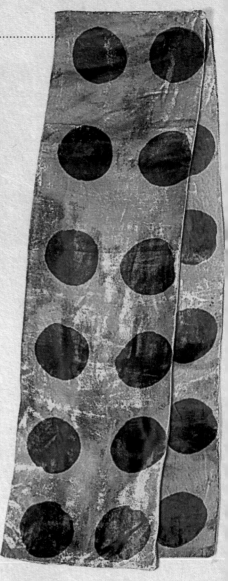

Now that you have tried out the basics of fabric painting and have realized the tremendous possibilities open to you, you can plunder the palette and wield your brush to indulge in a wild orgy of spots, swirls, and squiggles on your favorite fabric, whether it is a sheer silk scarf or a coarse canvas rug. Be inspired by these colorful creations to have fun and experiment with paint and dye.

▼ Rusty Pinstripes
To achieve its layers of colored stripes, the silk for this vest was folded, bound, and dipped in ferrous sulfate, then in indigo dye. Finally, it was pleated and painted with stripes of Fast Black K salt.

▼ Café Pillows
The text on these pillows is from a Dutch café menu, enlarged to different sizes on a photocopier. The lettering was traced onto the unbleached muslin over a light box, using green acrylic artist's color and an artist's brush.

de eerste verdieping is van 17.30 tot 22.00 uur als restaurant in gebruik.

belegde broodjes diverse salades vruchten & groente taarten.

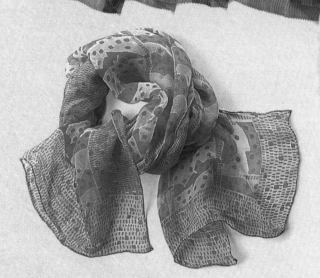

◀ Striking Spots
This boldly patterned silk velvet scarf was first handpainted using rich burgundy-colored, cold-water fiber-reactive dye to achieve a textured background, and then screen-printed on top with spots in discharge dye.

▶ Tiny Pleats
A length of silk organza was dyed with a combination of brilliantly colored acid dyes and discharge dye, then folded into many tiny pleats and dyed again for a multi-layered effect.

▲ Autumnal Shawl
Made from a square of delicate wool, this shawl was simply painted with bands of warm russet, orange, and brown acid dye. A large housepainter's brush was used to apply the different colors.

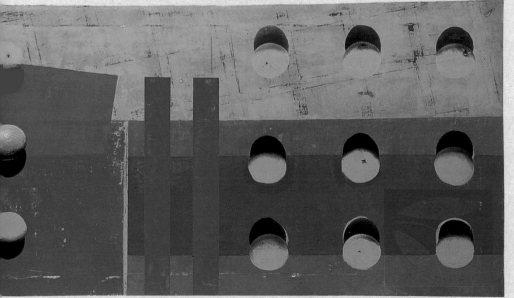

▲ Painted Chiffon
Plain cream chiffon has been transformed with the addition of orange and red acid dyes, painted in a busy pattern of geometric blocks and spots.

◀ Citrus Floorcloth
Inspired by oranges, this canvas floorcloth was first primed, then handpainted with oil paints; the oranges were screen-printed. A coat of varnish sealed the floorcloth.

◀ Sumptuous Squiggles

The vibrant patterning of squiggles, spots, swirls, and scribbly lines on this richly colored velvet scarf is made with discharge dye, using a combination of paintbrush and silk-screen techniques.

▶ Silk Dreamscape

A white silk comforter is painted with a mysterious landscape using cold-water fiber-reactive dyes mixed with thickener. The design is applied in several layers to achieve fine gradations of color.

▶ Hot Pink Satin

This square of fine silk satin was painted with a combination of cold-water fiber-reactive dyes and discharge dye mixed with color for some thrillingly unpredictable results. Masking tape was used as a stencil.

▼ Geometric Patterning

Solid squares and circles make up the ordered design on this velvet scarf. The background is first handpainted using cold-water fiber-reactive dye, then the shapes are printed with discharge dye and colored.

▶ **Medieval Influence**

Part of a magnificent wallhanging, this piece of natural silk was handpainted with acid dyes in printing paste, before being colored even more with stenciling and resist techniques.

▼ **Striking Silk**

This silk pillow is painted in bold colors for a strong impact. Acid dyes mixed with thickener, to prevent the dyes running, were applied using paintbrushes of varying sizes: a large rounded one for blobs, and a finer one for more detailed patterning.

▲ **Brilliant Bows**

These bow ties required careful planning to paint and make. Starting with a large piece of silk, and a limited palette of cold-water fiber-reactive dyes, an abstract design was painted on the fabric. The artist watched where the bows would appear in the finished fabric, which was then cut up and made into bow ties.

Printing

I F YOU WANT YOUR DESIGN to repeat all over
your fabric, or if you want to produce a set
of matching pillow covers, you will have
to master the art of printing. Silk-screen
printing is the most common method, and is by
no means as fearsome or highly skilled as people's
reverential awe of it might lead you to believe.
It is one of those skills that improves and
becomes easier with practice. Start
with something that is not precious,
such as cheap muslin pillowcases,
until you have mastered the business
of even pressure on the squeegee and
registering the different elements of your design.
If you cannot be bothered with frames and
squeegees, and all that cleaning up, you could
have cheap, innocent fun with a
potato. Potato prints do not have to
be rudimentary, and they can produce
a textile that glows with lively color and
radiating diamonds. Take a look
at spongeware china, which was once
printed with a potato, for inspiration.

Stenciled Heraldry

MATERIALS

Cotton fabric
Water-based screen-
printing inks
Precut stencils
or stencil paper

EQUIPMENT

Selection of sponges
Small dish
Absorbent fabric
Craft knife
Iron

INTENSE COLORS ARE USED for this prancing griffin: a slice of the spectrum – orange and red sponged onto yellow – for the background, while the heraldic beast itself is bright green in startling contrast. Scattered stars enrich the background, and an outline of gold holds the whole design together.

Other heraldic devices – such as shields, fleurs-de-lis, or rampant lions – lend themselves well to this treatment. There are plenty of books available on the subject, with lots of ideas for motifs and colors. Instead of the brightness of this particular version, you might prefer the subtle, faded look of ancient crests painted on castle walls. You could also look at favorite paintings for inspiration. Alternatively, since the technique of stenciling lends itself to large areas without too much difficulty, you might consider decorating a pair of curtains with geometric borders or an edging of rope swags and tassels.

This is an easy and effective project, with much impact for comparatively little effort. The heraldic griffin stencil, which is comprised of three different pieces, is probably its most complicated aspect.

Griffin Rampant
Look to royal weddings and coronations for clues to pomp and circumstance, or research your family coat-of-arms. Bold designs like this pillow look good in groups and can carry any amount of gold rope and tassel trim that you care to add.

Seats of Majesty
*With their vibrant colors and touches of gold, these
grand and exotic pillows could easily grace a maharajah's palace,
or be just the thing for a howdah.*

Sponging the Pillow

Sponging is a simple method of applying color to give a stippled texture. Here, sponges of different density are used to give solid or more open color.

Cotton fabric

Water-based screen-printing inks

Stencil

1 *Lay the cotton fabric on a work surface. There is no need to tape it down. Simply hold it in place while you colorwash the entire surface with diluted screen-printing ink. Dip a natural sponge in ink, blot off the excess on the edge of a saucer, then wipe the sponge over the fabric, pushing it away from you. Blot the fabric lightly with absorbent fabric, and let dry. Rinse the sponge.*

2 *Take a precut stencil or cut a stencil from stencil paper (rigid paper impregnated with linseed oil). Here, the stencil is of a griffin. Place it in the center of the dry fabric. Dip an open-textured sponge in orange ink, dab off the excess ink on a saucer, then dab it over the fabric, allowing some of the background color to show through. Blot the fabric with absorbent fabric. Rinse the sponge.*

3 *Using the same sponge, dab red ink around the edge of the damp fabric, leaving a "halo" of orange ink around the griffin stencil. Blot the fabric with absorbent fabric. Rinse the sponge; remove and clean the stencil.*

4 *Position the "negative" stencil (the stencil paper from which the stencil shape was cut in step 2) over the image on the fabric. Sponge green ink through the stencil. Blot the fabric, rinse the sponge, and clean the stencil.*

5 *Take a stencil of the outline of the griffin and position it over the image on the fabric. Using a close-textured synthetic sponge, dab gold ink through the stencil. (Using an open-textured sponge might make the line patchy.) Blot the fabric lightly with absorbent fabric, and clean the stencil.*

6 *Cut a stencil of a star, and using the same synthetic sponge as in step 5, dab gold ink through the stencil randomly over the fabric around the griffin. Blot the fabric lightly with absorbent fabric. Wash the sponge thoroughly and clean the stencil.*

7 *When the fabric is completely dry, set the screen-printing inks by ironing the fabric for 2 minutes with the iron on a hot temperature. The fabric is now ready to be made into a pillow.*

Leafy Sheer Silk

MATERIALS

4 tea bags
Soft water
Batik silk
Paper
Gold silk
outline marker
Press-print
Styrofoam
Gold acrylic
fabric paint

EQUIPMENT

Bucket
Rubber gloves
Iron
Frame
Thumbtacks
Pencil
Photocopier
Soft felt-tip pen
Craft knife
Printing roller
Paint tray
Masking tape

SOFT WATER AND TEA BAGS make a very basic formula that can rescue many a brash new fabric or print from too-bright whites or too-bold colors, all at war with one another. If in doubt, try a corner of your fabric before you commit an irreplaceable length. Having been toned down with tea, this silk is decorated with a delicate skeleton leaf using a gold outline marker, and the design is then built up with solid ash leaves printed in gold. The effect is refined and ethereal, and careful tracing is repaid by a convincingly professional finish. Because this is, in a sense, an organic design, which can be repeated with minor variations for as long as you have fabric, is is ideal for curtains or long, floaty silk skirts and shirts. An exact repeat is quite unnecessary; in fact, an element of randomness is part of the charm.

Any black-and-white design, however complex, can be enlarged and traced, and any simple outlined design can be block-printed. You could also explore different colors of silk dye and outliner to suit your taste and decor; try scarlet and gold on hot pink, for example, or an indigo night sky with gold and silver.

Floating Leaves
Translucent silk with a soft sheen and a sumptuous drape, treated with a random scattering of golden leaves, is perfect as light floaty curtains for summer, or in addition to heavier curtains for winter privacy. The silk was originally brilliant white, but the traditional trick of dunking it in soft water and tea gave it a subtle parchment color and a hint of antiquity.

Translucent Trio
Very different effects can be produced by changing the background color, the printing motif, and the color of the ink. A combination of tracing and printing, random or regular, can result in a loose romantic look or Bauhaus severity.

48

Decorating the Silk

This is your chance to explore three techniques —
tea dyeing, pen tracing, and block printing — all of which
can be combined to create something sizeable.

Batik silk

Tea bags

Soft water

Gold acrylic fabric paint
and silk outline marker

Press-print Styrofoam
and leaf pattern

1 *Place four tea bags in a bucket and half fill it with boiling soft water. Remove the tea bags after a minute. Wearing rubber gloves, immerse the silk in the liquid and swirl it around to ensure an even distribution of color. After 2 minutes, remove the fabric and iron it dry with a medium-hot iron.*

2 *Stretch the dyed fabric over a frame and pin it to the frame with thumbtacks. Find or draw an image that can be repeated on the fabric. Photocopy it to the required size and lay it underneath the framed silk. Using a gold silk outline marker, copy the outline of the image on the silk.*

3 *Fill in any details, using the silk outline marker, to complete the design. Here, the design is of leaves that are filled in with veins. Repeat the freehand drawing along the whole length of the silk.*

4 *Make blocks to print on the fabric. To do this, make a paper pattern of a leaf and draw around this on press-print Styrofoam using a soft felt-tip pen. Cut out three or four of these shapes with a craft knife.*

5 Using a pencil, gouge veins and other details in the Styrofoam blocks. Roll a printing roller in a tray of gold acrylic fabric paint, then roll it up and down over the Styrofoam block several times to load the block with paint, ready for printing (see inset).

6 Stretch the silk over a work surface and fasten down with tape. Press a printing block firmly on the fabric to print the leaf motif. Repeat to print more motifs. You will need to ink up the block after every one or two prints. Do not overload the block, or the print will smudge. Wash the block periodically; let dry before reusing.

7 When you have finished printing, iron each area of the fabric for 30 seconds, with the iron on a hot setting, to set the paint. Keep the iron moving constantly.

Easy Potato Print

MATERIALS
White cotton fabric
Water
Water-based screen-
printing inks
Medium-size potato

EQUIPMENT
Wash line
Clothespins
Housepainter's brush
Iron
Small paring knife
Paper towels
Thin, smooth
sponge cloth
Spatula

AS PRINTING EQUIPMENT GOES, you can't get much more basic than the potato. Whatever your experiences were in kindergarten, this project demonstrates that potato prints can be both fresh and sophisticated. The visual chemistry of the base and printed colors of this tablecloth sizzle wonderfully. You do not have to be Van Gogh to make your prints look good; you and your children can take turns on an equal basis.

The skill here, apart from coming up with a strong basic design and glorious color palette, is the clever cutting of the potato diamonds to give a perfectly interlocking pattern. This may take a bit of practice. For an all-over design, such as this one, regularity of printing is essential to ensure that the neat star and hexagon do not take on a life of their own.

If the prospect of making this tablecloth alarms you, you could try using the same technique to make a bedspread of rainbow patches with a more random print; make each patch no more than a manageable 6in (15cm) square. You could also start with a pillow cover and work up to a matching tablecloth.

Radiant Table
Even on a gray day, this starburst tablecloth pulsates with Mediterranean sunshine. The colors are from a clean, pure spectrum that will lift your spirits every time you look at them.
Lay your table beneath a canopy of vines, and you can dream yourself on a Greek island. Not many tablecloths can do this.

Star Turns
Diamonds – the basic block from which these designs are composed – may be a girl's best friend. But, if working neatly from the center seems beyond you, you could sprinkle your cloth with stars, squares, circles, hearts, or any other shape you can cut from a potato.

Painting and Printing the Fabric

First, dress in your oldest clothes and cover every surface with newspaper. Aim for a great casual sweep of color as the basis for your design. Then tackle your potato.

White cotton fabric

Water-based screen-printing inks

Water and potato

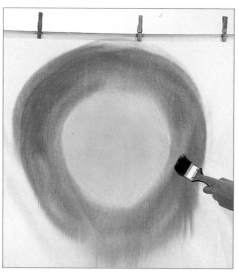

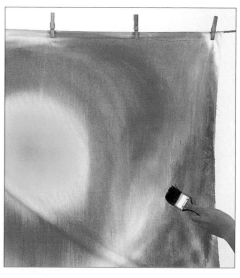

1 *Wash the fabric and hang it on a line with clothespins. Using a housepainter's brush, first dab dilute yellow, then red, screen-printing ink in a circle on the fabric. The colors will merge, creating a circle of orange.*

2 *Apply dilute pink ink on the corners and blue ink on the outer edges of the fabric. When the fabric is completely covered with ink, leave it to dry. Then press it with a hot iron to set the inks.*

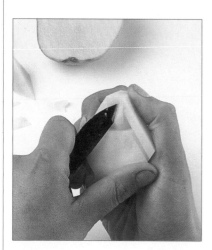

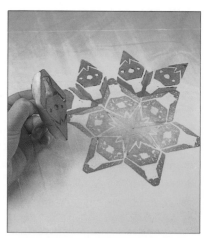

3 *Using a small paring knife, cut a medium-sized potato in half. Carve a design into one of the halves to make a printing block. When you print with the block, the raised areas will be visible. Blot the cut surface of the potato with paper towels to absorb any excess moisture.*

4 *Ink up a thin, smooth sponge by applying screen-printing ink onto its surface with a spatula, so the ink is absorbed into the sponge. You can apply more than one color on the sponge, as here, where the sponge is being inked up with yellow, pink, and red inks.*

5 *Press the carved half of the potato first onto the inked sponge, then onto the painted fabric, to make a print. Beginning first with yellow ink, start to build up a rosette design in the center of the fabric. Lift up the potato half carefully after each print to avoid smudging the ink.*

6 *Working around the central rosette, continue to build up the pattern using different colors. You will need to keep re-inking the potato block after every two or three prints. Press down hard on the potato to achieve a crisp, sharp print. If you find the potato becomes soft and the printed edges blurred, replace it with the other potato half, taking care to cut out exactly the same design as before.*

7 *Continue to build up the pattern, extending the rosette to the edges of the fabric. Change from one color to the next when you start a new circle. Here, blue changes to purple around the edge of the rosette pattern.*

8 *When you have completed the design, leave the fabric to dry for 24 hours. Iron it twice on the front and back with the iron on a hot temperature, to set the inks. The fabric is now ready to be made into a tablecloth.*

Silk Screen Shells

MATERIALS
Photocopied motifs
Acetate
Newsprint
Brown gummed strip
Cotton T-shirt
Water-based screen-printing inks
Water

EQUIPMENT
Photocopier
Black felt-tip pen
2 screens
Masking tape
Craft knife
Towel
Tablespoon
Squeegee
Sponge
Iron

EVERYBODY WEARS T-SHIRTS — they are the universal answer to everyday chic. It is surprisingly simple to customize a T-shirt to suit a particular person or occasion; anything that can be photocopied can be printed, with the size of image and the screen as the only constraints. A repeated motif, like the mermaid on this T-shirt, is a cheap way to make the best use of the process. The shell motifs came from a book of Victorian engravings.

Having fathomed the basic process of transferring sharp, graphic images to fabric, you can plunder myriad sources of black-and-white line drawings for images. Catalogs of typefaces, for example, can yield wonderful lettering, while reproduction Victorian catalogs contain everything from rutabagas to rowboats. The point about silk-screen printing is that, thanks to the availability of photo stencils, you can reproduce crisp, complex images and repeat them as often as you wish. Your entire clan could be clad in T-shirts bearing the family motto printed in red, black, and gold; or, you could decide to print a misanthropic Monday morning message with which to greet the world of work.

Shore Shirt
Nothing conjures up memories of the seashore like a clutch of bivalves and gastropods. These ones are beautifully detailed and elegantly arrayed around the neckline and sleeves of a plain white T-shirt.

Flurry of Color
Simple blocks of color, overprinted with a repeat motif, have a dramatic impact on a plain, long-sleeved top.

Printing the T-Shirt

Silk-screen printing is not a difficult technique to master.
Plain T-shirts are cheap and easy to get hold of, and come in
a rainbow of colors; just make or buy your screen (see
p.11) and enjoy yourself.

Cotton T-shirt

Photocopied motifs

Acetate and newsprint

Brown gummed tape

Water-based screen-
printing inks

1 *Arrange your photocopied motifs in a suitable design. Here, shell motifs are repeated to form a necklace. Photocopy the design on to acetate (see p.10) and touch up the copy with a black felt-tip pen. Take the acetate and a screen to a printer, who will transfer the design photographically on to your screen to make a photo stencil.*

2 *Once you have the screen with your photo stencil on it, you can create a paper stencil to use with it, which will enable you to print a background color before printing the outlines with the actual photo stencil. Tape newsprint over the photo stencil on the screen. Hold the screen up against a light source, and trace around the design with a felt-tip pen.*

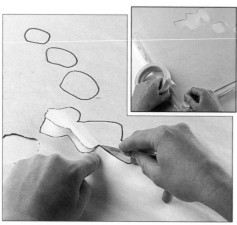

3 *Remove the paper from the screen and cut out the traced shapes with a craft knife. Keep the blade flat to avoid tearing the paper. Lay the second screen down so the mesh is in contact with the work surface; stick moistened brown gummed tape around the edges of the mesh and the wooden frame (see p.10). Turn the screen over; place the paper stencil on the mesh and tape the edges down (see inset).*

4 *Line the T-shirt with several layers of newsprint to keep ink from penetrating both layers of the fabric. Lay a towel and newsprint on a flat surface; lay the T-shirt on top and secure with masking tape. Place the screen on the T-shirt so the paper stencil is in contact with the area where you want to print the design. Spoon magenta ink along the top edge of the screen.*

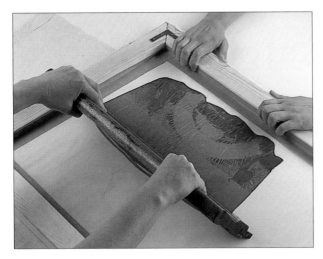

5 You may need the help of an extra pair of hands to hold down the screen frame as you print. Starting at the end farthest away from you, pull the squeegee (see p.10) firmly and evenly through the ink toward you. Carefully lift up the screen to reveal the printed image on the T-shirt. Wash the screen thoroughly using cold water and a sponge. If ink is allowed to dry on the screen, the mesh will become clogged and unusable.

6 Take the screen with the photo stencil on it and lay it down so the mesh is in contact with the work surface. Stick wet gummed tape around the edges of the screen mesh (see p.10). Position the screen over the T-shirt, making sure that the photo stencil aligns with the paper stencil image already printed. Spoon black ink on to the mesh, and pull the squeegee over the design as before to print the image. Wash the screen thoroughly.

7 Repeat the process to print further motifs, as required. Here, mermaid motifs have been printed to extend the undersea theme. Finally, iron the fabric for several minutes, with the iron on a hot setting, to set the inks.

Confetti-Bright Silk

MATERIALS

Paper

Silk satin crepe de
chine/georgette,
woven in stripes

Masking tape

Cold-water fiber-
reactive dyes

Linoleum

Discharge dye

EQUIPMENT

Pencil or paints

Absorbent fabric

Artist's brush

Steamer

Linoleum-cutting
tools

Printing roller

Paint tray

THIS SILK SCARF IS A SAMPLE of just about as many processes as possible on one piece of fabric. To start with, the silk crepe de chine itself has a luxurious satin stripe. This is then crosshatched with crisply defined sky blue lines, enlivened by a dazzle of freehand dots and squiggles, printed with a linoleum block, and bleached with discharge dye. With two steamings thrown in, you might justifiably feel somewhat daunted. But the finished scarf has irresistible delicacy and charm, and when taken individually, each stage is perfectly manageable. With so much going on in the design, it doesn't matter whether your stripes are straight or your squiggles are regular. The finished result is an allover pattern of great refinement, held together beautifully by the repeated linoleum-print pattern.

This project is a masterpiece to work up to when you have understood all the stages separately on other projects. The processes involved are too complex to apply to anything much bigger than a scarf, but the chosen fabric drapes in the most sensuous way, and the lively design would adapt equally well to a shawl.

Shining Stripes
Using a satin-striped fabric gives this scarf a head start. Unadorned, the fabric alone looks good, but its many layers of color and filigree of dark pattern raise it to family heirloom status. You could overpaint all sorts of patterns, from paisley to spots, on this scarf.

Fair and Square
The general principle of layers of color, stripes stenciled through masking tape, and a unifying print can be given endless subtle variations – no two scarves need ever be the same. Dyeing the base fabric is another possible stage, should you wish to add to the intricate patterning.

Painting and Printing the Silk

*This is a project that takes time and consideration.
Go slowly and don't panic – the linoleum print brings it
all together very effectively.*

Silk satin crepe de
Chine/georgette woven
in stripes

Cold-water fiber-
reactive dyes

Linoleum and
masking tape

Discharge dye

1 *Sketch or paint a design for the fabric on paper. Stretch silk satin over absorbent fabric on a work surface, and secure with masking tape. Tape strips of masking tape over the silk satin to create lines and blocks.*

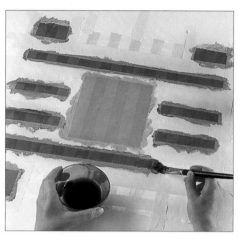

2 *Using an artist's brush and cold-water fiber-reactive dyes, paint stripes of color on the fabric. These colors will form the basis of the design, so they should be bold.*

3 *Remove the masking tape forming the resist pattern (see p.8), leaving the strips of tape around the edges. Build up the pattern in the undyed areas with squiggles, circles, and spots of color. Remove the fabric from the work surface; let dry, then steam for 20 minutes to set the dyes (see p.10).*

4 *Make a printing block with a small rectangle of linoleum. Use linoleum-cutting tools to gouge out the lines of the pattern, being careful always to cut away from you. When printing with the block, the raised areas will be visible, while the areas that have been cut away will not appear.*

5 Ink up the linoleum block by rolling a printing roller first in a tray of navy blue dye, and then over the cut surface of the linoleum. Press the block over the silk, then lift it carefully to avoid smudging the print. Continue to print until you have covered the silk. You may need to ink the block after every two or three prints. Let the fabric dry, then steam it for 20 minutes to set the dye.

6 Apply discharge dye on to the surface of the silk, to bleach the colors already applied and to create another layer of pattern. Here, the discharge dye has been blockprinted over the entire piece and painted in the center of the fabric to create an animal motif.

7 Set the discharge dye by steaming the fabric for a maximum of 10 minutes. The fabric is now ready to be made into a scarf.

Seashore Canvas

MATERIALS

Paper
Opaque photographic
liquid
Acetate
Cotton canvas
Brown gummed tape
Water-based fabric-
printing ink
Water

EQUIPMENT

Reference material
Pencils or paints
Photocopier
Artist's brush
Sponge
4 screens
Absorbent fabric
Masking tape
Tablespoon
Squeegee
Hair dryer
Iron

A NINE–PART PATCH PATTERN in four strong colors makes a good bold statement on the coarse canvas of this director's chair; the blue, tan, and gold recall the color of sand and sky. This design is an example of the power of restraint: four colors are about the most one can deal with comfortably using silk screens, and four colors are plenty for visual effect. This semiabstract design can be repeated endlessly in any quartet of colors you care to choose. Simplifying the design gives it punch; for example, you could use just the outline of the amphora. After all, there is no point in being delicate with a piece of furniture that is going to have to hold its own with the elements and cope with ice cream and suntan oil spills.

Experimentation in miniature with paintbox and brushes is a good starting point for many of the projects in this book. Use colored paper if you are considering using colored canvas. Faced with brand new jars of silk-screen ink, it is all too tempting to use them just as they come. When working small, it is easier to envisage the interesting subtleties achieved by mixing colors and using slightly offbeat shades.

A Seat for the Boardwalk
The glory of silk-screen printing is that you can repeat a pattern as often as you wish. In this case, if the passion strikes, you could make chairs for the whole family as well as a duffel bag from the same canvas.

Swinging Slings
Same design, different colors, and very different looks – these two seat slings for directors' chairs demonstrate how adaptable the method is, and how very easy it is to get a professional finish.

Printing the Canvas

Heavy canvas responds well to screen printing and takes color in a very satisfying way. Practice is all you need to achieve a smooth, even finish.

Acetate, paper, and opaque photographic liquid

Water-based fabric-printing inks

Cotton canvas

1 *Using reference material from various sources, make initial sketches of a design for your fabric. At this stage, it might simply be shapes or colors that provide inspiration. As you play with ideas, your design will gradually take shape.*

2 *After you have decided on an initial design, make photocopies of your sketches, simplifying them if necessary, and assemble them in a larger format. Here, tiny sketches form the basis for a larger design incorporating squares of abstract elements.*

3 *After the design is finalized, plan which colors to use. In screen printing, each color requires a separate screen (see p.10), so it is advisable to limit your color palette to four at the most. Choose colors that work well together. If you work out this stage accurately, it will be easier to prepare the acetate for the screens (see p.10).*

4 *Using opaque photographic liquid, trace each color of the design onto a separate sheet of acetate. Use an artist's brush for fine linework, or a sponge for a mottled effect when covering a large area. Take these four sheets of acetate, together with four screens, to a printer who will make a photo stencil on each screen (see p.10).*

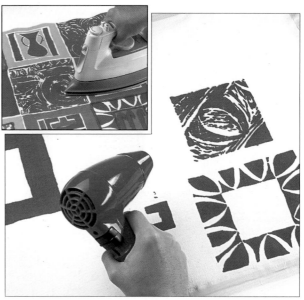

5 *Stretch a piece of cotton canvas over absorbent fabric on a work surface and secure with masking tape. Stick wet brown gummed tape around the edges of the mesh and the wooden frame on each of the four screens to make sure that excess ink does not seep through the mesh. Position the first screen on the fabric. Spoon fabric-printing ink along the top edge of the screen, and pull the squeegee (see p.10) through the ink toward you to print the design on the fabric (see p.59). Wash the screen with a sponge and cold water.*

6 *Dry the fabric with a hair dryer before positioning the next screen. Repeat the printing process with the three remaining screens, aligning them accurately each time (see p.10). When you have printed all the colors, dry the fabric with a hair dryer, then iron it for several minutes, with the iron on a medium temperature, to set the inks (see inset).*

7 *The printed fabric is now ready to be used. Cotton canvas is tough and sturdy, and is an ideal fabric for making into chair covers or bags.*

Marbled Silk

MATERIALS
Cold-water fiber-
reactive dye
Silk satin crepe
Water
Paper
Acetate
Brown gummed tape
Printing dye paste
Discharge dye

EQUIPMENT
Rubber gloves
Bucket
Pencil
Scissors
Masking tape
Photocopier
Screen
Tablespoon
Squeegee
Sponge
Steamer
Iron
Protective mask
Laundry detergent
Fabric softener

THIS OPULENT SILK SATIN SCARF combines stormy dark green and purple, with paler ripples of bleached-out color. The swirling pattern is complicated to reproduce, but the finished result is well worth the effort. The simple trick of turning the photo stencil and using it twice makes for a very effective marbled design. You could even research the patterns and colors of genuine marble for more inspiration.

Discharge dye is a substance that is exciting and somewhat unpredictable in its effects; by bleaching out areas, it provides a quick way of enriching the design and giving it an extra rhythm. Here, the tones are very close so the finish is subtle and stippled. You could experiment with colors that make a more emphatic contrast, or possibly with different tones of the same color for a stylishly understated look. There is no limit to the number of layers of color you can apply, simply by shifting the photo stencil slightly each time. An allover textural effect like this can be used successfully on large pieces of fabric – taking great care with registering the edges (see p.10) – which you can use to make anything from curtains and pillow covers to vest fronts.

Moody Colors
This discreetly sophisticated scarf is printed with perfect offbeat winter colors in a design that has an even, professional air; it would make a fitting partner to fine leather and silk tweeds.

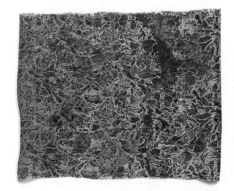 

Rich and Rare
These muted earth and sunrise colors in silk satin and gauze are reminiscent of the psychedelic abstracts of long ago, but are infinitely more refined. When you have grasped the principle of marbling, the entire spectrum is yours to exploit.

Printing the Silk

*Silk-screen printing becomes easier the more you do it.
Start with expendable fabrics, and work up to sumptuous
crepes and satins.*

Silk satin crepe

Repeating design

Cold-water fiber-
reactive dye and
printing dye paste

Discharge dye and
brown gummed tape

1 *Mix dark green cold-water fabric dye,
following the manufacturer's instructions.
Wearing rubber gloves, dip the fabric in the
dye for an hour, keeping the fabric moving
constantly to ensure an even distribution
of color. Rinse the fabric in hot, then cold,
water until the water runs clear, then let dry.*

2 *Make a repeating design for the fabric
by cutting vertically and horizontally
through a busy rectangular-shaped pattern
and transposing the cut sections (see p.10).
Make several photocopies of the design; tape
the photocopies together to make one large
continuous pattern. Photocopy this on to
acetate (see p.10), and take the acetate with
your screen to a printer, who will make a
photo stencil (see p.10).*

3 *Once you have the screen with the photo stencil on it,
moisten brown gummed tape and stick it around all
four edges of the mesh and the wooden frame to prevent
any excess dye from seeping down the sides of the mesh
and possibly ruining the fabric.*

4 *Secure the dyed fabric to the printing surface with
masking tape. Spoon purple dye paste on to the top
edge of the screen, and print the design on the fabric (see
p.59). Repeat the printing process along the fabric, being
careful to match the design as you go (see p.10).*

5 *When the fabric is dry, steam it for 20 minutes to set the dye. Then wash it in warm water and leave to dry again. Turn the fabric 180° so the design is facing downward, and tape it down on the surface again. Position the screen on the fabric, directly above the printed image. Spoon discharge dye along the top end of the screen mesh (see inset), then print again (see p.59). Printing on top of the first upside-down print will add texture to the design. The discharge dye is similar to a bleaching agent: it takes out the ground color in the fabric. It will not immediately be visible on the fabric; it will simply look wet.*

6 *Allow the fabric to dry, then iron it for a few minutes to bring out the discharge dye, keeping the iron moving constantly to avoid marking the fabric. The areas where the discharge has come into contact with the fabric will be lighter, creating subtle patterns. As you iron the fabric, you will see the image slowly appear. The longer you continue to iron the fabric, the stronger the effect of the discharge dye will be. The hot discharge dye can produce an unpleasant smell; either work in a well-ventilated area or wear a protective mask.*

7 *Wash the fabric in detergent and fabric softener, and either let it drip dry or iron it dry. The fabric is now ready to make into a scarf.*

Ideas to Inspire

Here is a collection of different techniques and interpretations to make your fingers itch to start painting. Dreamed up by the brightest talent in textiles, it shows every kind of printing, from sophisticated potato patterns to the most complex mixes of silk screen, discharge, and overlays with hand-coloring. Printing lets you repeat patterns, and using photographic methods, you can replicate fine graphic detail. So experiment and enjoy yourself!

▶ **Sketched Pillows**
A combination of screen printing, appliqué, and machine embroidery was used to produce these two pillows. Screen printing was used to decorate the background; both the lettering and the scribbling on the cow were sketched onto the screen. Then appliquéd motifs were stitched on and details embroidered.

◀ **Printed Plant Life**
Made from a length of silk crepe, this herbaceous fringed scarf was screen-printed with a resist medium. It was then embellished even more by hand-painting discharge dye on top.

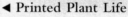

▶ **Bulldog Bonanza**
Made from silk satin, this canine scarf was screen printed with several colors of acid dye, which were then subdued with an overprinting of sepia.

◀ **Zigzag Prints**
A palette of blue and orange is the basis for this printed coverlet. The rows of zigzag potato prints are echoed by the base colors to create a rhythmic repeat design.

72

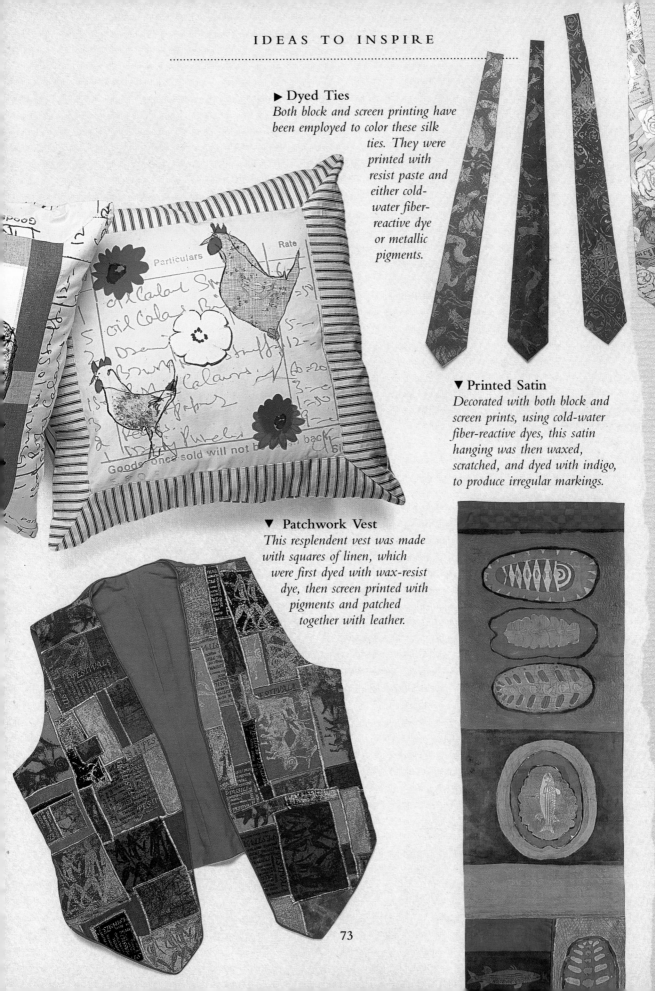

▶ Dyed Ties

Both block and screen printing have been employed to color these silk ties. They were printed with resist paste and either cold-water fiber-reactive dye or metallic pigments.

▼ Printed Satin

Decorated with both block and screen prints, using cold-water fiber-reactive dyes, this satin hanging was then waxed, scratched, and dyed with indigo, to produce irregular markings.

▼ Patchwork Vest

This resplendent vest was made with squares of linen, which were first dyed with wax-resist dye, then screen printed with pigments and patched together with leather.

◄ **Scarf of Many Colors**
Using a combination of resist dyes and cold-water fiber-reactive dyes, this silk satin crepe and georgette striped scarf was screen-printed and then overprinted to create layers of color and texture.

► **Overlapping Patterns**
This silk chiffon fabric was screen-printed using cold-water fiber-reactive dyes, then overprinted with both plain and colored discharge dye. The screen was rotated each time to create overlapping areas of color.

◄ **Blue Pineapple Scarf**
Several shades of blue were used to color this crepe de chine fabric. It was first handpainted with cold-water fiber-reactive dye, then the pineapple motif was screen-printed on top. A light blue pigment dye was then screen-printed on the fabric to create more detailing.

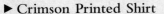

▶ Crimson Printed Shirt

The silk was first dyed with red cold-water fiber-reactive dye, then the design elements — the stripes and horse motif — were screen-printed with cold-water fiber-reactive and discharge dyes. The yoke and pocket were printed separately.

▼ Clock Prints

These silk scarves were dyed with deep blue cold-water fiber-reactive dye, then sections were handpainted with discharge dye. Finally, clock images were screen-printed on the silk using navy blue and beige pigment dyes.

◀ Good Fronds

A fern frond was used as a stencil for these pillow covers. It was held in place over unbleached muslin, and the muslin roughly painted with a mixture of blue and green water-based fabric paint, applied with a large brush.

Gutta and Wax-Resist

....

GUTTA AND WAX are used to control color on fabric. They form an impenetrable barrier to the liquid dye, trapping it within their confines. The line you draw with the gutta does not have to be thick, but it does have to be complete; color will escape through any gaps. The final result will always have a hint of the leading in stained glass windows – which are a good source of inspiration – although you can match your gutta to your fabric paint to reduce the impact of the outlines. It is essential to plan your design, and either trace it on fine silk or draw it first with an auto-fade pencil, so you can apply the gutta with decisive strokes. Gutta does slightly modify the texture of silk, although it will soften with washing and ironing. The wax used for batik is removed completely by ironing and does not affect the feel of the fabric.

Glowing Squares

MATERIALS

Silk satin
Gutta
Silk paints

EQUIPMENT

Wooden frame
Silk pins
Soft pencil
Ruler
Gutta applicator
bottle
Hair dryer (optional)
Artist's brush
Iron

AS BRIGHT AS THE ROSE WINDOW in Chartres Cathedral, this pillow cover is as easy to make as painting by numbers, and the results are far more glorious. The fine gutta outlines suit the discipline of the design and become an important element in the finish. You can buy gutta (a thick liquid which creates a barrier to contain paint) in a range of colors, as well as clear; black outlines would emphasize the stained-glass look.

If you have a steady hand, you could plagiarize direct from postcards of your favorite high altar, or take ideas from the strong motifs of medieval heraldry. Twentieth-century painters, including Joan Miró and Roy Lichtenstein, lend inspiration for this crisp graphic style allied with primary colors. For a less regimented, looser approach, you might search the library for reproductions of Paul Klee's work, and experiment with the more subtle and muted colors of his palette. Whatever idea appeals, it would be wise to practice using gutta on some spare fabric before you commit yourself on your square of unsullied silk; there is not a lot you can do about mistakes, and on a geometric design, such as this, they will show.

Bright and Beautiful

Edged with painted pennants, and backed by somber black silk, this pillow has a way of making its presence felt. The edging does not need to have a lining – the gutta seals the fabric so it does not fray.

Square Dance
A cubist bull's-eye of concentric squares that positively pulsates with color, in vibrant contrast with a classic op-art eye-dazzler in black and white.

78

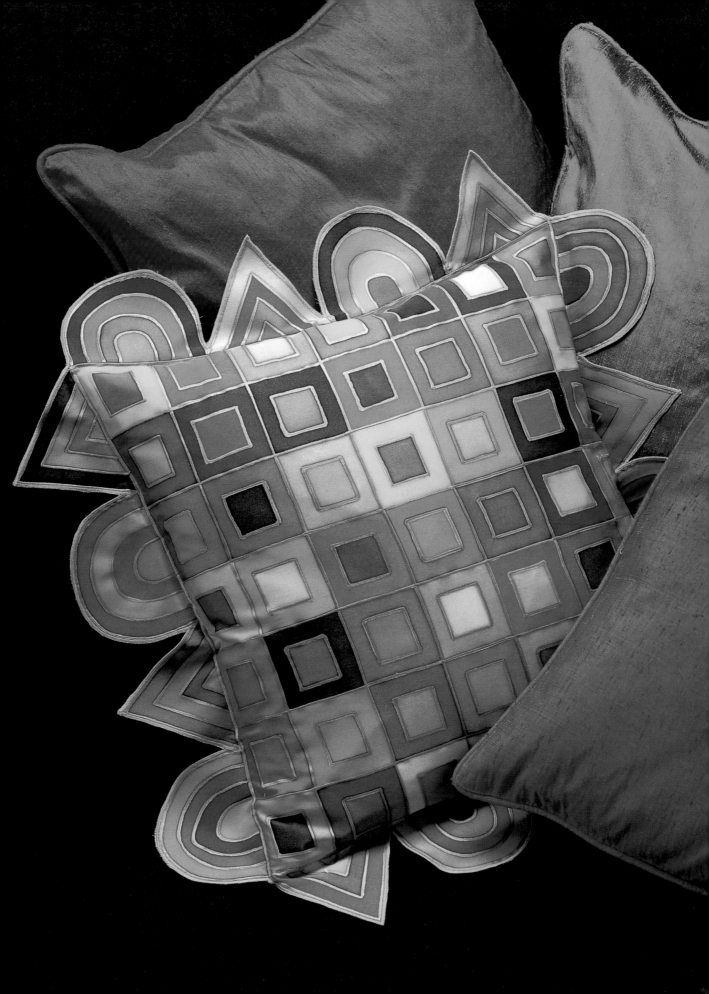

Painting the Silk

Pinning the silk is the only tedious part of this project –
the actual painting is instant enjoyment.

Gutta and silk satin

Silk paints

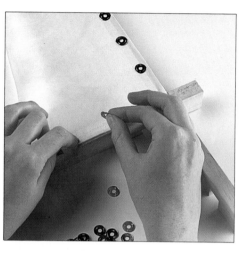

1 Stretch a piece of silk satin over a wooden frame. Starting at a corner of the fabric, pin the selvage side of the silk to the frame with three-pronged silk pins. Pin at 1in (2.5cm) intervals down each side of the fabric in turn, making sure that it is stretched taut.

2 When the fabric is pinned down on all four edges, draw your design onto the silk with a soft pencil; use a ruler for straight edges. Here, the design is geometric, with squares, arches, and triangles.

3 Hold the gutta applicator bottle vertically over a penciled line on the silk, and squeeze it so the gutta flows on to the fabric in an even line. Follow all the pencil lines with gutta, taking care not to smudge them. Let the gutta dry for about an hour, or dry it with a hair dryer for about five minutes. The gutta is dry when it feels hard to the touch; if it feels tacky, it is not dry yet.

4 Using an artist's brush, apply silk paints on to the silk. The paint will spread quickly over the fine fabric, and only stop when it reaches the gutta line, which contains it. Using one color at a time, paint shapes in each part of the silk, so the colors are spread evenly throughout the design and are not concentrated in one area.

5 *Continue to apply paints to fill in the shapes on the silk. If a color leaks through the line of gutta, apply gutta on top of the leaking color to prevent spreading. When the gutta is dry, paint over the leak with a darker colored silk paint to disguise it. Alternatively, dilute the leak with clean water and absorb it with a paper towel.*

6 *Continue to build up the colors and pattern to complete the design. Because the silk paint is fairly dilute, it soaks into the fabric immediately, so there is no need to wait for one color to dry before applying the next. Be careful not to place the same colors in adjacent shapes. Keep an eye on the overall balance of color as you go.*

7 *When you have finished painting, let the silk drip dry for an hour, or speed up the drying time by using a hair dryer. When the silk is completely dry, iron it on the reverse side for two minutes to set the colors. The silk is now ready to be made into a pillow cover.*

Tropical Seascape

MATERIALS

Prerolled silk crepe
de chine scarf

Water-based silk dyes

Dilution fluid

Alcohol-based
gutta

Salt

Isopropyl alcohol

EQUIPMENT

Claw pins

Wooden frame

Three-pronged
silk pins

Sponge brush

Artist's brush

Gutta applicator
bottle with small
nozzle

Cotton swab

Steamer

G UTTA RESIST, A LIQUID THAT BLOCKS and contains the flow of paint, is a wonderful medium for controlling the colors in silk painting, but as in drawing, the neatness, thickness, and color of the line are all crucial aspects of the finish. The gutta barrier does not have to be thick, but it needs to be applied with a steady hand, so the line is graceful and the ends meet.

Much of the delicacy of this pattern derives from very fine outlines, meticulously drawn with gutta using a draftsman's pen nib. The swirling abstraction of the design comes from first flooding the crepe de chine with color, which results in the familiar balance of spontaneity with formality that is so often the formula for success. The drifting colors on the silk, reminiscent of tropical waters, owe their harmony to the fact that they are very closely related. Simple dilution of the silk dyes is one of the methods used to obtain variations, while salt and alcohol are used to give the color rhythm and liveliness. With all these techniques, practice will improve your touch and give your work a looseness and fluency.

Watercolors
Painted with the aqueous blues and greens of palm-fringed atolls, this is more than a mere scarf. The dreamy colors evoke a holiday in paradise, and it would make a generous and life-enhancing present for a sun-starved friend.

Shapely Fronds
These sinuous shapes of fern and seaweed are carefully drawn against a softly blurred background. Each of these variants is composed with a limited palette or four or five colors at most, and is all the better for it.

Painting the Silk

*This project combines the exuberance of sponge
painting with the intricacy of fine gutta lines. Sprinkled salt
and drops of alcohol enhance the design.*

Prerolled silk crepe de
Chine scarf and alcohol-
based gutta

Water-based silk dyes

Salt, dilution fluid, and
isopropyl alcohol

1 *Using claw pins, pin a silk scarf to a
wooden frame at intervals along the length
of the silk, using three-pronged silk pins at
the frame edge. The scarf should be stretched
taut. Dilute silk dyes with dilution fluid,
following the manufacturer's instructions.
Then, using a sponge brush, apply diluted
pale blue dye in patches across the silk.*

2 *Using an artist's brush, apply darker blue
dye in random patches across the scarf,
leaving light blue shapes in between. Apply
only a small amount at a time because the
dye quickly spreads across the fabric. Let the
fabric dry completely.*

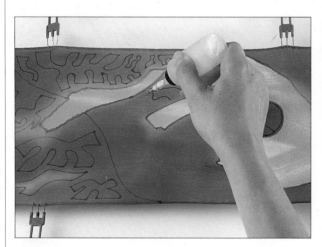

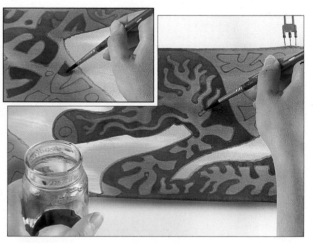

3 *Using a gutta applicator bottle with a fine nozzle,
apply a line of gutta around the pale blue shapes to
outline them. Divide the fabric into diagonal sections with
more lines of gutta. Draw shapes in the dark blue areas
of the scarf, leaving the pale blue shapes empty.*

4 *Working on alternate diagonal sections, paint over the
background with dark blue-green dye so the patterned
gutta shapes are pale in comparison. In the adjacent
diagonal bands, fill in the gutta shapes with dark blue-
green dye, leaving the background paler (see inset).*

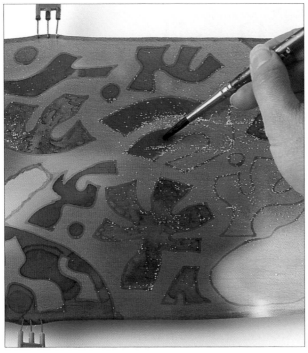

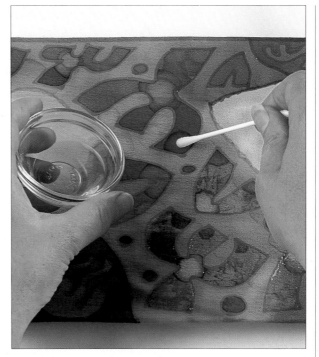

5 *To give the design added texture and interest, sprinkle salt over the shapes in some of the diagonal areas before applying the dye. Then, when you paint on the dye, the salt will draw it in different directions to create a pretty, feathered effect. Repeat this technique as often as you like along the length of the scarf.*

6 *Dilute isopropyl alcohol to the ratio of 1:1 with dilution fluid. Dip a cotton swab in the diluted alcohol, then dab it on parts of the painted design. The alcohol reacts to the dye by pushing it away to create interesting rings of color.*

7 *When the silk is completely dry, set the colours by steaming the silk for approximately 2 to 3 hours (see p.10), depending on the dyes used. Then dry-clean the silk to remove all traces of gutta from the fabric. The silk scarf is now complete and ready to wear.*

Aquatic Batik

MATERIALS

Cotton fabric
Wax (a mixture of
beeswax and paraffin)
Fabric dyes

EQUIPMENT

Frame
Thumbtacks
Pencil
Double boiler
Tjanting (batik pen)
Paintbrush
Artist's brush
Rubber gloves
Dye bath
Newsprint
Paper towels
Iron

A S WITH GUTTA RESIST, much of the quality of using wax to block dye depends on fineness of line and fluency of drawing. Patience is a very useful attribute for this, as is a clear idea of what you want to achieve. You can plagiarize from whatever sources are useful, but do make a few sketches and practice using the *tjanting* (a pen like instrument with a container to hold liquid wax) first. It would be a good idea to start with a simpler subject – this magnificent fish is painted with the skill and confidence that is developed over time. For the novice, the border alone would be a triumph.

The otherwise controlled, formal, and beautifully drawn design seems to gain from the unpredictable webs of inky blue obtained from crumpling the fabric in the dye bath. The dark lines and splatters are in keeping with the subaqueous subject, giving the fish a liveliness and coherence, but this stage could be omitted for those who prefer their fish unsplattered. The highly intricate border enhances the design and frames it beautifully. Look at Indian miniatures and Russian icons for inspiration on colors and subjects.

Waxworks
A fish this spectacular deserves a place of honor – it is far too splendid to be designated anything less than a work of art. Painted on fine cotton fabric, the colors look wonderful lit from behind; the technique could be used successfully for lampshades or blinds.

Fish for Compliments
Subtle variants on a piscatorial theme, these cavorting carp are delineated with exquisite attention to detail – every nuance of fin and gill is drawn with perfect fluency and rhythm.

Painting the Fabric
Approach this project slowly – exploiting the potential of layers of color requires careful planning.

Cotton fabric

Wax (mixture of beeswax and paraffin)

Fabric dyes

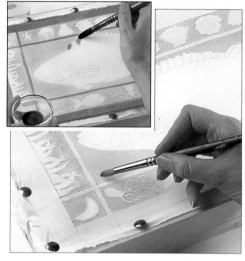

1 *Stretch cotton fabric over a frame, attaching it to the frame with thumbtacks. Draw a design on the fabric with a pencil. Here, the design is fish and shells. Melt some wax in a double boiler until it becomes liquid. Dip a tjanting (batik pen) into the hot wax to fill the container. Using the tjanting, apply hot wax over the penciled lines on the fabric, moving smoothly and slowly for an even line.*

2 *Fill in larger areas of wax using a paintbrush. Any areas that are waxed will resist the dye and will remain the colour of the fabric. Then, using fabric dye and an artist's brush, apply the palest colors on the design (see inset). Here, the border of the design and the head of the fish have been painted pale blue. Let the dye dry.*

3 *Using a tjanting, apply wax over the dyed areas where you want the color to remain. Here, wax has been applied to outline the fins of the fish and parts of the border.*

4 *Using an artist's brush, build up more colors on the design. When you are satisfied with the elements of the design, paint wax over them so the colors cannot change.*

5 *Using the tjanting, draw rows of tiny scales in hot wax on the body of the fish. By this stage, most of the fabric will be covered in wax.*

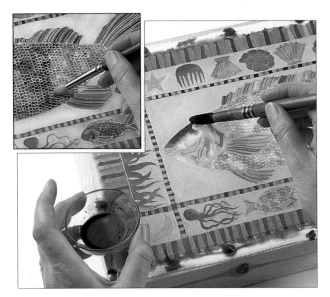

6 *Paint darker colors on some of the remaining unwaxed areas of the design. Here, the seaweed at the edges of the design and the fish's head are being painted dark greeny blue. When you have finished painting the fabric, brush wax over the design (see inset).*

7 *Remove the fabric from the screen. Then, wearing rubber gloves, immerse the fabric in a dye bath of dark blue fabric dye. Hold it in the dye for 10 seconds or so, then lift it out, place it on newsprint, and allow to dry, wiping off excess dye with a paper towel.*

8 *With the iron on a medium setting, iron the dry fabric between sheets of newsprint to remove the wax. Place paper towels over the front and back of the batik to prevent newsprint from transferring. The heat of the iron will melt the wax into the paper. Continue ironing until there are no more signs of wax. Ironing will not remove 100 percent of the wax, but a sufficient amount to make a batik suitable to be framed as a picture.*

Ideas to Inspire

Using gutta or wax-resist creates sharp edges in your design. Because of this, resist methods are favored by painters who enjoy fine detail, but they can also be used to much bolder effect in large, colorful designs, as seen here. So, aim high, prime your tjanting, grab your gutta, and start to paint.

▶ **Fruit, Flowers, and Fish**
A trip to Guatemala provided the inspiration for this colorful painting (right), while underwater swimming was the source of its companion (below). Both were painted on silk habutae using silk paints and colorless gutta.

◀ **Brilliant Color**
Realistic subjects depicted in vibrant colors are the hallmarks of this artist's work. Working on white silk, using acrylic-based silk paints and gutta, themes range from wild animals on a vest (left), to vivid vegetables (below) and fish and flowers on ties (right).

▲ Pictures and Cards
The fabric in these pieces was colored using the batik technique. Wax outlines were drawn onto the fabric (silk for the picture, and cotton for the greeting cards) with a tjanting, then silk paints were painted on the fabric in between the wax lines, using a brush to blend the colors for a more painterly effect.

▶ Geometric Design
This striking chiffon scarf is an example of the effectiveness of simple patterning that can be achieved using gutta. It has been painted with squares, triangles, and circles of solid color using silk paints. The narrow gutta outlines divide and emphasize the different areas of the design.

◀ Rainbow Scarf

Exploiting the colors of the spectrum to the fullest, this vibrant silk scarf is painted with a dazzling selection of silk paints in a pattern of diamonds, blocks, and swirls. The lines of gutta define the shapes of the design.

▲ Paisley Designs

Inspired by Indian wood-block designs, these patterned silk scarves were colored using batik. First, wax outlines were drawn on the fabric using a tjanting, then cold-water fiber-reactive dyes were handpainted in the unwaxed areas.

◀ Batik Bluebells

A woodland glade carpeted with bluebells is captured in batik. The use of wax and dye creates subtle highlights and depths of shadow not seen in other methods of fabric painting.

▶ Painted Motifs

Resist techniques have been used here to paint motifs on silk. A design of stars, circles, and dots adorn one scarf (above), while stylized flowers and leaves are painted on the other (right).

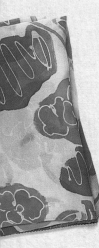

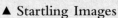

▲ **Startling Images**

A fantastic female form and floating feathers decorate these two crepe de chine scarves. The backgrounds were painted with a dilute wash of silk paint using a sponge brush, then the designs were drawn with gutta and painted with silk paints.

▶ **Floral Feast**

Delicately painted using hot wax applied with a tjanting, and a range of fabric paints applied with a fine artist's brush, this batik flower picture demonstrates the vast amount of detailed paintwork that is possible with this method of fabric coloring.

Contributors

The Author
p.40 centre

Philippa Bergson
p.92 top left and bottom right
Tel: 01986 784337
Church Cottage
Cookley, Halesworth
Suffolk IP19 0LW

Kate Blee
pp.18-21; p.39 center left
Tel: 0171-354 8676
182 Highbury Hill
London N5 1AU

Johanna Brinkworth
pp.78-81
Tel: 01257 277766
81 Weldbank Lane
Chorley
Lancashire PR7 3NN

Alison Britton
p.91 top right
Tel: 01365 324499
The Buttermarket
Down Street
Enniskillen, Co Fermanagh
Northern Ireland BT74 7DU

Kirstine Chaffey
pp.26-29; p.75 top right
Tel: 0181-287 5228
16a Morley Road
East Twickenham
Middlesex TW1 2HF

Maria Chambers
pp.52-55; p.72 bottom left
Tel: 01373 832076
Park Barn Cottage
Corsley, Nr Warminster
Wiltshire BA12 7QH

Philippa Crawford
pp.40-41 top; p.41 bottom left
Tel: 0131-557 0109
26 Drummond Place
Edinburgh EH3 6PN

John Everden
p.92 top right
Tel: 01782 644011
52 Parkway
Dairyfields, Trentham
Staffordshire ST4 8AG

Jane Fox
pp.56-59
Tel: 01273 608174
19 Rochester Street
Brighton
East Sussex BN2 2EJ

Jane Hickman
pp.86-89; p.93 bottom right
Tel: 01568 760461
Rose Villa
Poplands Lane
Risbury, Nr Leominster
Herefordshire HR6 0NN

Rachel Howard
pp.72-73 top
Tel: 0181-986 9889
22 Thomas House
Morning Lane
London E9 6LB

Clarissa Hulse
p.39 top right; p.72 center
Tel: 0171-916 4640
Studio W11
Cockpit Yard Workshops
Cockpit Yard
Northington Street
London WC1N 2NP

Claire Jobson
p.73 bottom left
Tel: 01325 481969
20 Linden Avenue
Darlington
Co Durham DL3 8PP

Jane Keeley
p.75 bottom
Tel: 01273 683610
54 Maseking Road
Brighton
East Sussex BN2 4EL

Louise Kilner
pp.68-71
Tel: 01203 417223
18 Roman Way
Finham, Coventry
Warwickshire CV3 6RD

Alexandra Lacey
p.41 top right
Tel: 01600 890958
The Thatch
Coppett Hill
Goodrich, Ross-on-Wye
Herefordshire HR9 6JF

Fiona Layfield
p.72 bottom right
Tel: 0171-336 7832
Unit 361
Clerkenwell Workshops
27 Clerkenwell Close
London EC1R 0AT

Helen Leaver
p.73 bottom right
Tel: 01772 39365
25 Coniston Drive
Walton-le-Dale, Preston
Lancashire PR5 4RN

Jacky Linney
pp.14-17
Tel: 01986 784402
Holly Tree Farm
Walpole, Halesworth
Suffolk IP19 9AB

Maggi MacNeill
pp.48-51
Tel: 0141-429 7279
12 Maxwell Terrace
Glasgow
Strathclyde G41 5HT

Kim Meyer
p.90 bottom
Tel: 0171- 209 3450
Studio 6, Cockpit Workshops
Cockpit Yard
Northington Street
London WC1N 2NP

Trisha Needham
*pp.22-25; p.39 center right; p.41
bottom right; p.91 bottom*
Tel: 0171-274 4116
Clockwork Studios
38B Southwell Road
London SE5 9PG

Jenny Nutbeem
pp.30-33; p.38 top left
Tel: 01728 668624
Boxers, North Green
Kelsale, Saxmundham
Suffolk IP17 2RL

Ruth Pringle
pp.44-47
Tel: 01242 604233
The Studio
Sudeley Castle, Winchcombe
Gloucestershire GL54 5JD

Mandy Pritty
p.38 bottom left
Tel: 0171-249 0038
76 Carysfort Road
London N16 9AP

Nahid Rahman
p.38 top right
Tel: 0956 324626
Broadway Studios
28 Tooting High Street
London SW17 0RG

Victoria Richards
p.74 right
Tel: 0171-737 8009
3 Clockwork Studios
38 Southwell Road
London SE5 9PG

Rosi Robinson
p.92 bottom left
Tel: 01444 471584
High Pines
Hundred Acre Lane
Wivelsfield Green
East Sussex RH17 7RS

Lichen Rowson
p.74 bottom left
Tel: 0171-794 3761
Flat 4, 52 Crediton Hill
London NW6 1HR

Hilary Simon
pp.90-91 top
Tel: 0181-672 2714
5 Charlmont Road
London SW17 9AL

Lucie Simpson
p.40 bottom; p.75 center
Tel: 00353 5661804
The Crescent Workshop
Castle Yard, Kilkenny
Ireland

Sally Weatherill
p.73 top right
Tel: 0171-249 0828
22 Carysfort Road
London N16 9AL

Isabella Whitworth
pp.82-85; p.93 top
Tel: 01235 527636
4 Kingfisher Close
Abingdon
Oxfordshire OX14 5NP

Sophie Williams
pp.34-37; p.40 top left
Tel: 0171-639 7524
91 Lausanne Road
London SE15 2HY

Hilary Windridge
pp.60-63; p.74 top left
Tel: 01286 673482
4 Bryngwyn Terrace
Ceunant, Caernarfon
Gwynedd LL55 4RH

Alexandra Woods
pp.64-67
Tel: 01252 621044
Drey House
Queen Mary Close, Fleet
Hampshire GU13 8QR

Natalie Woolf
pp.38-39 bottom
Tel: 0113242 2297
10 Wharfedale Street, Leeds
West Yorkshire LS7 2LF

Index

A
acid dyes 6, 18, 22, 34
aquatic batik picture 86-89

B
batik 9, 86-89, 91-93
blinds 14-17, 86
block-printing 73
    linoleum 9, 60-63
    potato 9, 43, 52-55, 72
    press-print styrofoam 9,
        48-51
bold felt blocks rug 22-25
brushes 7, 8

C
canvas 9, 39, 64
chairs 9, 64-67
chiffon 39, 74, 91
color
    lightfast 7
    spread 7, 77, 81
comforter 40
confetti bright silk scarf 60-63
cotton 6, 9
    painting/dyeing 14
    resist techniques 86-89, 91
    screen printing 44, 52, 56,
        64, 75
crepe 60, 68, 72, 74, 82, 93
curtains 48-51, 68

D
discharge dyes 34, 39, 60,
    68, 72
dyeing see painting and dyeing

E
easy potato print tablecloth
    52-55
equipment 8-9

F
fabric
    paints 6, 9
    preparation 8
    types 9
feathers 6
ferrous sulfate 30-33, 38
fiber-reactive dyes 6, 26, 60, 68
fixing 6-7, 9, 11

G
georgette 60, 74
glowing squares pillow 78-81
greetings cards 91
gutta 7, 9, 77-85, 90-93

I
indigo 30-33, 38, 73
ironing 6, 77, 89
isopropyl alcohol 85

J
jousting jumbos tie 26-29

L
leafy sheer silk curtains 48-51
lightfast color 7
linen 6, 9, 73
linoleum block 9, 60-63

M
marbled silk scarf 68-71
materials 8-9
muslin 14, 38, 75

N
natural fibers 6
nylon 6, 9

P
paint 6-7
painted jungle blind 14-17
painting and dyeing
    blind 14-17
    pillows 34-38, 41
    rug 22-25
    scarves 18-21, 30-33, 62,
        74, 75
    ties 26-29, 41
    vest 38
pens 8, 50
photocopied designs 10, 11,
    28, 38, 56
pictures 86-89, 90, 91, 92, 93
pillows
    gutta resist 78-81
    painting/dyeing 34-37,
        38, 41
    screen printing 44-47, 68,
        72, 75
pins 8
potato printing 9, 43,
    52-55, 72
preparations 8
press-print styrofoam 9, 48-51
primer 7, 39
printing 9, 43-75
    linoleum block 9, 60-63
    potato 9, 43, 52-55, 72
    press-print styrofoam 9,
        48-51
    silk screen 9-11, 43-51,
        56-59, 64-75

R
rayon 9
registration marks 10-11, 68
repeat patterns 11, 43, 60, 70
resist techniques 9, 30, 41,
    72, 73
    gutta 7, 9, 77-85, 90-93
    wax 7, 9, 73, 77, 86-93
rugs 22-25

S
safety 6, 7, 8, 34
salt 30, 33, 38, 85
scarves
    linoleum block 60-63
    painted and dyed 18-21,
        30-33, 39, 40, 75
    resist techniques 82-85,
        91-93
    screen printed 68-71, 72, 74
screen printing 9-11
    chair 64-67
    curtains 48-51
    pillows 44-47, 72
    scarves 40, 68-71, 72, 74, 75
    shirts 56-59, 75
tie 26-29, 73
vest 73
seashore canvas chair 64-67
shawls 39, 60
shirts 56-59, 75
silk
    linoleum print 60-63
    painting/dyeing 18-21, 26-
        33, 38, 40-41, 75
    paints 6, 9
    resist techniques 78-81,
        82-85, 90-93
    screen printing 48-51, 68-
        71, 72, 73, 74, 75
silk screen 9, 10-11
    see also screen printing
silk screen shells T-shirt 56-59
sponges 7, 9, 46, 82
steam-fixed dye 6-7, 9, 11
stenciled heraldry pillow
    44-47
stencils 9, 10
    see also screen printing
stylish striped silk scarf 18-21

T
tablecloth 52-55
tea bag dye 48, 50
techniques 10-11
thickeners 7
throws 22, 22-25, 72
tie-dyeing 30-33, 39
ties 26-29, 41, 73, 90
tjanting 9, 30, 86, 92, 93
tools 9
tropical seascape scarf 82-85
T-shirt 56-59

V
velvet 34-37, 38-40
vests 38, 73, 90
viscose 9

W
wallhangings 41, 73, 90
water-based paint 6, 9
wax resist 7, 9, 73, 77, 86-93
wool 6, 9, 22, 39

Acknowledgments

Sumptuous is a fair description of all the fabrics that make up this book – watching textile artists at work is a thrilling vision of pure creativity, and every one of the many contributors has had insights and ideas enough to deserve a weighty monograph of their own. They tackled the formidable logistics required for step-by-step photography with fortitude and intelligence and the results of their labors should convince the most sceptical Philistine that a thing of beauty – especially if you can wear it – is a joy forever. And they made it all so simple. The mind-boggling task of orchestrating this array of talent fell to Heather Dewhurst. As before, she has proved herself not only to be an infallible human computer with more bytes than you've had hot dinners, but also calm, capable, and fun to work with. Clive Streeter excelled at photographic aerobics and sped up and down that ladder as though Jane Fonda was on his tail. Despite toiling well beyond the call of duty, he kept us giggling and every picture attests to his skill and inventiveness. Andy Whitfield plied everyone with essential nutrients and kept everything working. Ali Edney produced inspired props to make the finished fabrics look as splendid as they deserved, and Marnie Searchwell took the whole complicated cocktail of words and pictures (every detail of which she subjected to the most maddening and punctilious scrutiny) and turned it into a book of which we are all proud. With such a team and such a glorious subject, producing this book has been pure pleasure. Finally, of all the many people who advised, the staff at George Weil in Hanson Street deserve very special thanks.

The following companies kindly loaned props for photography:

Candle Makers Supplies
28 Blythe Road
London W14 0HA
Tel: 0171-602 4031
Artist's materials and fabric dyes

Cowling & Wilcox
26-28 Broadwick Street
London W1V 1FG
Tel: 0171-734 5781
Artist's materials

Farrow & Ball
33 Uddens Trading Estate
Wimborne, Dorset BH21 7NL
Tel: 01202 876141
"Old White" matt emulsion paint on pp.49 and 87

Liberty
Regent Street
London W1R 6AH
Tel: 0171-734 1234
Bowls on p.31; silk cushions on p.79

Liberty Furnishings
3 Chelsea Harbour Design Centre
London SW10 0XE
Tel: 0171-349 5500
Cotton chenille fabric on p.79

Phillips Carpets
250 Staines Road
Ilford, Essex IG1 2UP
Tel: 0181-507 2233
Sea grass matting on pp.35 and 57

Purves & Purves
80-81 & 83 Tottenham Court Rd
London W1P 9HD
Tel: 0171-580 8223
Glassware on p53

James Smith & Sons
Hazelwood House
53 New Oxford Street
London WC1A 1BL
Tel: 0171-836 4731
Umbrella on p.69

Spread Eagle Antiques
8 Nevada Street
London SE10 9JL
Tel: 0181-305 1666
Silver box on p.61

Stuart R Stevenson
68 Clerkenwell Road
London EC1M 5QA
Tel: 0171-253 1693
Japanese brushes on p.31

The V & N
29 Replingham Road
London SW18 5LT
Tel: 0181-874 4342
Gilt curtain pole supports on p.49; French metal chairs on p.53

George Weil and Sons
18 Hanson Street
London W1P 7DB
Tel: 0171-580 3763
Artist's materials and fabric dyes

Winsor & Newton
51 Rathbone Place
London W1P 1AB
Tel: 0171-636 4231
Artist's materials